STICK-SEASON GROUSE

STICK-SEASON GROUSE
And Other Stories of Hunting, Fishing, and Dogs

—TED ROSS—

With a Foreword by Peter Miller

SILVER PRINT PRESS
COLBYVILLE, VERMONT

Copyright © 2004 by Ted Ross

Pandamonium. First published as *Teaching an Old Campaigner* that appeared in *Spaniels in the Field*, Spring, 1988 and in *Obituary*, Fall, 1995, also from *Spaniels in the Field*.

Should We Take the Clay Shooters Hunting? was first published in *Shotgunner Magazine*, Spring, 1983. The excerpt by Emerson Hough first appeared in *Out of Doors*, 1915.

Barry and Quinn. Scroll of Honour is from Talbot Radcliff, Presaddefed Estate, Wales, UK. with permission from the Radcliff family.

A Woodcock Memoir, by A. Ross Jones, was first published in *The Bulletin*, 1972 and is reproduced with permission of his estate.

Slick Henderson's list on page 98 is from *Baja Oklahoma*, by Dan Jenkins, ©1981 Simon and Shuster

The Twilight Season, by Peter Miller, was first published in *Sports Afield*, October, 1978 and is reprinted with permission of the author.

Getting Together was first published in *Spaniels in the Field*, Spring, 1993.

Tree Houses refers to a story by Dana Lamb in his book *Beneath the Rising Mist*.

Same Sex Union and Dog Ownership was first published in *The Vermont Eagle*, April, 2000. Peter Miller's reply is reprinted with permission of the author.

On Dogs and Dying contains stories by Maurice Chambers (*Our Last Talk*) and Charlie Rose, Wildrose Shorthairs (A prayer), reprinted with permission.

All rights reserved under International and Pan-American Copyright Conventions. No part of this book may be reprinted without express permission from the publisher.

Published in the United States by Silver Print Press, 20 Crossroad, Colbyville, VT 05676
Cover Photograph by Peter Miller
Foreword by Peter Miller
Illustrations by Paula Rembisz
Design by Peter Holm, Sterling Hill Productions
Printed in the United States by Maple-Vail
First Edition, September, 2004

Publisher's Cataloging-in-Publication Data:
　Author: Ted Ross. Ill. By Paula Rembisz
　Title: Stick-Season Grouse and Other Stories of Hunting, Fishing and Dogs
　Published: Colbyville, VT; Silver Print Press, 2004
　Collected stories by Ted Ross on his hunting, fishing and dog experiences that take place in the American West, the South, New England, Canada and England.
　Subject:
　　650.7 Hunting
　　650.7 Fishing
　　650.7 Dogs
　　651.7 Vermont
　144 p. ill, 184 pages, 152 x 228 cm.
　Library of Congress Control Number; 2004108321
　ISBN: 0-9749890-2-9 (Hard Cover) 0-9749890-3-7 (Soft Cover)
To order books singly or in bulk, contact info@silverprintpress.com. 802.244.5339.
Website. www.silverprintpress.com.

This Book is dedicated to Spaniels Tweeds I-IV

Contents

Foreword / ix
Preface / xii
Acknowledgments / xiii

1. Stick-Season Grouse / 1
2. There Is No Such Thing as a Good Fly-Fishing Dog / 6
3. For Mearns I Yearn / 9
4. The Stonefly Sagas / 13
5. Bathtubs on Anticosti Island / 24
6. The Twilight Season / 27
7. Chester Weir(d) / 40
8. The Cruelest Month and Falling In / 44
9. The Next One / 51
10. Barry and Quinn / 53
11. Pandamonium Chronicles / 58
12. Feist Dog Squirrels / 64
13. Should We Take the Clay Shooters Hunting? / 69
14. Horror Moving / 74
15. Fishing Buddies / 78
16. English Barney / 81
17. Field Trials and Tribulations / 85
18. The Last Grouse on Pea Pond Road and Woodcock Memoir / 89
19. Drinking with Dogs / 98
20. Tree Houses / 102
21. Same-Sex Union and Dog Ownership / 107
22. Travels with Tweed IV / 112
23. The Duck in the Fireplace / 127
24. The Great Vermont Capon Hunt / 130

25. Three Camps Plus One / 134
26. On Dogs and Dying / 147
27. "Getting Together" / 154
28. Death of a Woodcock Cover and Leaving Vermont / 157
29. Not Martha Stewart's Kitchen / 160

Afterword: Storing Lasts / 163

— Foreword —

I can't classify this book. It fits on the far side of the normal pattern of hunting and fishing literature. Do you know anyone who would write such chapters as; "Drinking with Dogs," "Same Sex Union and Dog Ownership," or "The Great Vermont Capon Hunt"?

The ethics, morals and passion of hunters and anglers run deep and they often develop into a philosophy grafted onto their psyche. I know hunters and anglers whose prime consideration is the number of birds they kill or big fish they land. To others the sport is a social activity, no different than playing golf to butter up business clients or show off at their club. Then there are the lyrical types, and if they turn to writing about their sport, their prose is close to purple and they tilt their writing to people of their social background, a mélange of Abercrombie and Fitch and *Hunter's World* stereotypes.

Ross is different; the stories in this book are flavored by a split personality that is two-thirds Vermont woodchuck and redneck and one-third landed gentry. Ross was born into the Social Register. He went to St. Paul's Preparatory School, about as upper crust as you can get. He graduated from Union College and followed the debutante balls up and down the East Coast. He joined the Marines and regrets that he never was in combat. He hired on as an advertising salesman for the hook-and-bullet and ski magazines and finalized sales at golf clubs, private hunting and fishing camps and on the ski slopes. He plays the piano and has done so in nightclubs. He reads more than he watches television and is familiar with the best writers. Although he respects, as he says in one story, the writer Dana Lamb, who hunted in the New York township in which Ross grew up, his favorite is Ivan Turgenev. He founded the *Rossfalloon* in Nova Scotia, a most unusual fishing club (private, no women ever allowed, and that too is a special chapter in this book), and there on the mantelpiece is a Tanqueray bottle which, when Ross dies, will be filled with his ashes. He named his kennel Liver's End. He is old fashioned; he does not know how to use a computer and never sent an e-mail.

Ross is talented and smart. He has a quirky humor and, like most salesmen, knows the latest jokes. He is uncannily gifted as skier and an able tennis player and has taught these sports for a living. As with so many of us, he was introduced to hunting and fishing by mentors. Through the years he developed his skills in fly-fishing and wing shooting and became a successful dog trainer and sometime field trial judge. You will find, in a number of chapters, that he campaigns Springer Spaniels.

He is also a champion drinker—of multiple martinis, Newfoundland Screech rum, cheap sherry—and proud of it. It is a sight to see Ross raise his head in a duck blind, as the sunrise, mirrored off his red face like a beacon, flares all incoming ducks.

Although Ross is a traditionalist and an elitist he also carries within him the persona of a good ole boy. His hunting and fishing dress is casual shabby, and who would ever expect that a person so clothed would be shooting with a custom-built Holland and Holland 20 bore and has a Bentley in the garage? He is as at ease with an English lord at his hunting estate in Wales as he is with some Mississippi or Texas country boys. Most everyone except AAs and feminists like Ross, although he is so far on the right he would fit right in at some Southern Baptist cookouts. He has the knack of making friends with locals and is held in some awe by Nova Scotia companions and guides—perhaps for the large amounts of alcohol he can consume, or his reputation as a superb

Foreword

chef. He has roots in Newfoundland and, as the last of the line in the States, is looking up lost relatives in that province. He likes all things cod and it is a tradition for him to cook codfish cakes on the opening day of bird season.

For part of the year Ross lives in Texas in a trailer permanently dimpled by egg-sized hail. Another of his campers, this one named *Stonefly*, survived a dozen round-trips from Vermont to Montana. Ross is, for all intents, broke with no fat bank statement; he lives on pensions, social security and what he derives from guiding with his dogs. He should sell the Bentley. He gambles at black jack and on stocks. He wins, he loses, he drinks more martinis, he hunts and fishes. He is deeply hurt by the loss of a dog. He is divorced and lives alone, although that is a misconception, because his dogs are always by his side or on his bed, and he talks constantly to them and kisses their snouts.

Why all this talk about the writer rather than the stories? Well, only Ross could come up with such commentary on our field-and-stream culture. He is going on sixty-six and these stories represent an outdoor life style that is shrinking, particularly here in Vermont.

Ross has the curiosity of a journalist. This book describes diverse people and places from the sanctified eastern private clubs to a good ole boy Mississippi camp, a young trainer in England, and guides in Nova Scotia. He rants occasionally about how women morphed men's clubs, about liberals like me, but enjoys most people whom he meets in the field. He doesn't write rapturously about the experience as much as about the people, and he takes an essayist point of view at the social implications of the sport.

He does so with an Edwardian view; he was born in the wrong century.

Peter Miller
Colbyville, Vermont, 2004

— Preface —

The Devil stopped by for one of his infrequent visits recently. He apologized for his truancy, saying he was as busy these days year-round as Santa is Christmas Eve, what with all the liberal politicians to tempt and the tininess of their souls.

He presented a canned pitch tailored for aging sportsmen and prepared by his PR department. He touted his success rate, particularly with heavy drinkers over sixty years old who may go at any time.

The offer is simple and direct; I could commence a new life in this brand new millennium with a lifespan equal to or greater than what my current total will be. At the end of which I will belong to him, which is probably the case anyway. The catch is that I would have no memory of my current life.

I turned him down flat. If not a sportsman, I might have taken his offer.

— Acknowledgments —

Many people named and unnamed shaped my life and directed me on a path of dogs, hunting, fishing and drinking. I owe special thanks to all these who have touched my life:

My parents and family (all deceased) who provided a first rate education for an indifferent student, especially my grandmother, Katharine Humes, who also taught me what southern cooking is all about.

Wilson Lloyd, who with his dog, Nod, taught me something about bird hunting and to never, never be without a good dog.

Dana Lamb is an author whom I greatly admired as a lad, and whose style I sometimes try to emulate.

John Scott Jr., Bullet Shih, Graham Hall, Peter and Briggs Forelli and some of their friends who allowed me to assume a mentoring role without the expense of being a father. Now they are all in their thirties.

Members and welcome guests of my fishing club in Nova Scotia have provided me with camaraderie and support in my dotage.

Rodman K. Tilt, who gave me my first publishing job in 1965 as an advertising salesman for *Sports Afield*. He was also a second father and companion afield and his spirit remains with me. And John Scott Sr., who risked hiring me on five different magazines spanning three decades.

Pondview Kennel's Jerry "Ray" Cacchio and Dan Lussen, whose excellent advice over twenty-five years has helped me to become a fair dog trainer. Also I thank those clients and field trialers whom I met there and who became friends.

The Mashomack Club in Pine Plains, New York.

Dan Daly (deceased) and David Thieringer, the support crew, guides and members who continue to provide enjoyment and income for me and my dogs.

Andrea McKnight, who transformed the bangings on my 1950 Smith Corona into a legible manuscript.

Lamar Underwood, the youngest editor *Sports Afield* ever had, and who has since written and assembled many books, for his support and advice on the final manuscript of this book.

Peter Miller has hunted and fished with me over two score years. He claims to be a much better woodcock shot than I, a master at sleuthing out woodcocks from a cover, but he's not much good at training dogs and doesn't drink as much as he should. He can photograph, write and edit, as he has with this book, but that's all he can do.

And I should take a bow to any ancestors for passing on the right sort of genes to act out a gentleman's life without the large bank account.

There are many others, but lastly I wish to thank Mr. Tanqueray and Ms. Bombay for stimulating my creative abilities and my fondness for memories.

Stick-Season Grouse

— 1 —

MOSCOW, VERMONT • DECEMBER 2000

Stick-Season Grouse

It is a firm conviction grouse should never be hunted seriously until the leaves are completely down. In this neck of the woods that means Halloween or later. The leafers have headed down to New Jersey along with the woodcock, and the deer hunters don't go into the woods for rifle season for two weeks. I haven't been deer hunting since 1974 so during this time I duck hunt, staying out of the woods to respect their hunt as much as for the safety of me and my dogs.

The reason I don't purposefully pursue early grouse is also out of respect . . . for the quarry. For sure, if one presents a "gimme" flushed from a hedgerow into an open field, I'll take it. But grouse in heavy cover are a risky business. My dogs have found too many cripples left by others in the thick stuff for me to think otherwise. Half the time you just cannot tell if you have hit them. If hit lightly they run and hide, the hunter gives a cursory search and the game is left to die slowly or wait for the fox.

The sparser the cover the farther from the gun the birds flush. I switch to 6s during stick season, killing grouse often at extreme range for a 20 bore. But I can see them fall as can the dog, greatly enhancing the chances of bringing the bird to bag.

I disagree with many of the experts who espouse creeping through the woods and stopping at every bush to make a skulking bird nervous enough to break cover. This may work for the dogless hunter in thick early cover, but later birds are better walked up at a normal pace for you and your dog. As winter approaches grouse move distances on wing and leg, taking advantage of late food sources not yet covered by snow and ice. I clipped an article years ago that gave a partial list of preferred grouse forage. Besides the obvious poplar buds, beech nuts and apples there are exotics such as possumhaw and wintergreen. Study the next grouse tracks you find in early snow—they go every which way, simulating a "herd" of grouse. Most likely it is one bird gathering widely. Points or close flushes on these birds are rare. A large percentage of food for these late loners is in trees, which is the most difficult flush of all. The rule for pointers or flushers is Work close!

Rarely do you encounter concentrations of late-season birds, but in a particularly succulent food patch this can happen. High bush cranberries that hold their fruit late are irresistible to grouse, and you could luck out.

Two seasons ago during December I was hunting with my English Springer, Samantha. She is not my best bird finder, but she is the luckiest. Take Samantha on a hunt and game materializes. We approach a strip of cranberry and as she enters the covert a grouse flushes from the tallest twig and flies right at my head. St. Vitus, the grouse hunter's patron saint, dictates that you ignore the oncoming shot or the one directly overhead and jump around to take the bird going away.

My first shot is over; you have to shoot below the feet on this one. I correct and puff it in the open field with the second barrel.

Samantha now at hup in the covert and I with empty gun watch nine more birds escape their banquet to the high pines across the meadow. The next year this covert was subdivided and developed.

Autumn 2000 is a strange one. Reports confirm a paucity of grouse in Vermont and most of New England with glowing exceptions from pockets in inland Maine where a few hunters report the best ever. Against all odds amongst declining federal counts and poor seasons since 1997 the coverts that I hunt in Vermont were as full of woodcock as in the 1960s. This could be misleading as I did not sample the covers throughout the thirty-day season but concentrated during a few days in mid-October. Many northern coverts were barren so I journeyed to the southern counties for a two-day hunt with Jerry. We may have hit the timberdoodle lottery by catching the entire flight going south at once. In all the coverts visited I have yet to hear a grouse flush, let alone see one.

The self-imposed hiatus I observe during deer season is in effect until the Monday following Thanksgiving. I can amuse myself with the incredible maneuvers by the desperate Gore minions attempting to find a Florida judge to appoint him president, and duck hunts.

Just in . . . a report from the Miller brothers. These thirty-year-olds hunt on foot, loathe to employ the Jap revenge for the *Enola Gay*; the ATV. They went far into a wilderness area seeing everything but a harvestable buck including four moose, one huge; two mature coyotes; a three-hundred-pound black bear in the apples and twenty grouse flushed from high beeches.

Grouse Diary 2000

November 28th — weather cool and gray with light winds from west. Location Northeast Kingdom of Vermont. Joined Roger for a late mallard shoot on Connecticut River. After lunch below old family farm in linear hunt along unused railroad tracks with high bush cranberries throughout. Roger constructs a semi-dry blush wine from these of pleasing flavour and potency. Usual number of flushes in an hour hunt—six. This year—two. My spaniel, Arrow, flushes one that flies into contiguous pines. No shot. Then a small hen down the tracks presents rare open shot. Retrieve accomplished with some difficulty. Then half a mile back along the ties. Bog along both sides hid several flushing mergansers which we let go as they taste like hot anchovies.

December 16 — copious rain in Scotland, howling wind in Iowa, back in Vermont. Waterbury Center thirty degrees and rising with a southern front moving in, heavy rain forecast. Six inches fresh snow on the ground. Covert varied with ample apple and poplar buds and sumac berries. Fruit rotting on the ground. No grouse. Arrow flushes white phase snowshoe hare. Chases, stops on whistle but don't risk a shot. She just won a ribbon at the National Amateur Championship and this isn't the U.K., where spaniels are trained on fur and feather. I shed a tear ... jugged hare, yum! This is the back end of an overgrown farm I hunted three decades ago. The orchards that still produced fruit then could provide twenty or more flushes. Coyotes, development and snowmobile trails have worked their black magic. But nothing, where are the birds? Last hunted with Henry whose family cares for Arrow, two years ago same time of year. No snow, sunny, negligible wind. One bird missed flushed overhead off cliff (8th station high house) and a pathetic miss in open out of the sumac where we pushed the hare today.

Stick-Season Grouse

December 23 — bitter cold and clear. Moretown, Vermont, with Peter and Mildred the shorthair. This is extremely thick in the early season, in fact unhuntable. A long uphill to pines at top. There is a food source along the ridge that attracts one bird. Mildred points off the logging road, the bird runs and makes the same mistake several of its predecessors have made at the same spot and Peter's 16 gauge Parker speaks, Mildred out and back and bird in the coat. Nothing is in the usual thickets but as we walk downhill through the pines birds start flushing overhead. Occasional glimpses but never a shot. At least half a dozen. Though late afternoon it is early for them to roost. Spruce buds are not a ruffed grouse's favorite, particularly with so many other delicacies readily available. There is no wind from which they need shelter. Grouse know no rules.

December 27 — stop in New York State on way south to Texas for one last hunt with John Y. and Mildred. This covert has everything in abundance as well as views across the Hudson to the Catskills and Taconics. Wonderful stone walls crisscross the fields and are laced with gray osure whose small berries are a grouse magnet . . . usually. One lone bird flushes wild. John, who is a conservation officer, says this is a typical year two thousand grouse experience, but the wild turkeys are so numerous we see sign and scratching everywhere. We make a joke about grouse after millions of years suddenly becoming migratory, and I wrap it up for another year.

— 2 —

CAPE BRETON ISLAND • JULY 2003

There Is No Such Thing as a Good Fly-Fishing Dog

Early in dog ownership I read or heard this. I hope it was not the title of another article.

Like many who crave dog company, I refused to believe this. I was flush with success at having trained (or should say overtrained) my first acceptable spaniel; I followed an English regimen heavy on obedience work boring the poor animal stupid before he even saw his first game bird. He would sit unmonitored for hours, heel over burning coals and despite all this, ended up a fair bird dog. Certainly, I reasoned, he would be a fine companion on trouting expeditions.

He dutifully sat watching me from the bank of Vermont's Lamoille River. It was late July; the light at dusk was soft, the hay a just-cut fragrance and I was casting a size 14 gray dun. One of the river's legendary browns rumored to feed once a month at full moon on swimming field mice rose off the bottom and hooked itself—my largest trout ever on that sultry evening in 1965.

Characteristically it did not jump but fought my 5-weight Orvis bamboo with head shakes, runs and sulks on the bottom.

The tussle was dogged, but finally he was winched into the shallows and started to thrash for his life. A brown and white streak went past me and pounced on my fish. Line, leader, trout and spaniel became a single blur. The trout was free and the spaniel was wrapped in line, hook imbedded in an ear. Nothing fights harder than a hooked guide except a hooked dog. The only way this scene could have been worse would be if the dog had done this to a total stranger.

Over the years I have developed a credo that if the dog does not add anything to the party, leave it kenneled at home. I allow latitude in these guidelines: front-seat riding, beach time, non-hunting hikes, cross-country skiing and even golf if playing alone. But never fly-fishing. I need to concentrate on the river, not on the dog around or in it. A well-trained animal in a canoe on a pond might work in my dotage but has yet to be tried.

The problems relate to the similarities between fishing and hunting. We don specific clothing and footwear carrying tools and gear. We seek prey. It is too much for the canine brain to differentiate between the two. Dogs think they are hunting and behave accordingly. Yet dog owners insist on bringing their hunting pals to the river.

Henry, a friend and salmon fishing icon to some, has purchased a Visla to be his companion through his late seventies. Even more painful than his tales of this miraculous creature's prowess on woodcock, which I must seriously question, is Buck's behavior on the river to which his master insists on bringing him. Despite futile whistle blowing and invective the brute barks and runs the bank. His owner and I are on a collision course; it is only a matter of time. Joe the guide sang out across the river from the shingle to the high bank where Henry was hideously perched, "Henry, that dog is going to take five years off your life!"

"Joe, he has already taken ten!"

And twenty off the other poor anglers subjected to this charade. I know of one exception: a veterinarian from Prince Edward Island whose dog is a paragon of streamside deportment. A big, calm Black Lab of devoted demeanor, for hours he sits on the bank watching his master. He is petted and praised by other anglers, but I submit risk lurks when a hooked twenty-pounder starts splashing in the shallows.

— 3 —

TUCSON, ARIZONA • FEBRUARY, 2001

For Mearns I Yearn

Great howling Gods! What kind of weather forecast is this? South Texans proudly call this season Winter-Spring. Vermonters would call it "mud season." The temperature is thirty-something under gray moisture-filled skies with more of the same ahead for the entire week. A phone call to friends, Dave and Gary, AKA Mearns Man, in Arizona confirms the best year for Mearns Quail in recent history.

The 1976 Shasta trailer that once served as singer Roy Clark's dressing room—he signed the kitchen counter for the former owners, is mud stuck. There is no hope of moving it to the quail lease until the ground dries, so there will be no Texas quail hunt. Leighton, for whose guiding service I work, gives me leave and his blessing. Our Texas quail are drowning.

Dogs Mildred, Tweed, and Arrow, along with shooting gear and golf clubs, are loaded in our nine-passenger 1987 Olds Custom Cruiser and we are off. The trip to Tucson requires two days and spans some of the most desolate country in the United States. Many miles parallel the Rio Grande. The Mexico side bears little resemblance to the Texas side; gaily painted shacks are stacked on top of each other and separated from the next settlement by one hundred miles of nothing. Hills not thought of as part of the flat Texas landscape rise out of prairie, embracing modern day ghost towns. Endless freight trains pass through scrub dotted with cattle. Comfortable with my own company and used to isolation, this country unsettled me. Far from threat or anxiety, I sense ennui. Historical markers commemorate legendary cattle drives; the constant wind pushing tumbleweed is as haunting to me as it must have been to those heroic drovers.

The Mearns Quail is an elusive and regional species that was briefly on the endangered list. They are found only in a corner of Arizona, New Mexico and a tiny dot in Texas. Also called Harlequins, these clown-faced quail are shy, secretive and virtually impossible to find without a close-working pointing dog; shorthairs are preferred. These birds catapult rather than flush. They scratch for food like tiny turkeys with oversize feet on powerful legs. Wing-size to body-size ratio is greater than the Bobwhite, so the bird is even quicker off the mark. Water requirements are supplied by their food sources, allowing the Mearns to live in high desert. Finding water will not guarantee finding birds. Covey sizes are small—a dozen is huge, four to six the norm. They have a reputation for holding tight, but when hunted they learn to bust wild and disappear without a trace, frequently burying in the grass and letting the wind wash their scent.

Word has spread. Because of the long season and glowing reports put out by the state on the Internet, multiple out-of-state rigs with trailers housing a dozen dogs are frequent specters. Some arrive without places to hunt or guides booked. I wish them no luck and a swift return home. These birds have been hunted and stressed to death. If not content with finding a few coveys and bagging a couple birds a day you shouldn't be here.

Dave, my host, is an estimable Lab trainer, a transplant from the East to Arizona whose curriculum vitae include: helicopter door gunner in Vietnam, finish carpenter, machinist, cowboy, ranch foreman, land speculator salesman and house renovator. He made the move after the only twister in the recorded history of Duchess County, New York, hit his kennel, scattering expensive client dogs but killing none. He found them all over several weeks, but figuring his luck was running low, he sold out and relocated as a partner ranch manager. His only dog is Dorothy, the pit bull. Afflicted with brain stem atrophy she jerks and dances like a marionette on speed. She finds a kindred soul in my Tweed, whose back legs collapse, causing him to topple. When they play it is a parody of a Fred and Ginger routine.

Gary—*Mearns Man*—is also multi-faceted; local cowboy, carpenter, hunter, guide, what little luck he possessed ran out a few years back. His life litany trumps even the most mournful cowboy ballad. "If I bought a pumpkin farm, they'd cancel Halloween." Since my previous visit he had contracted a virus that destroyed his heart muscle. Fifty-plus cowboys with a fondness for saloons and hard labor are not placed at the top of the heart recipient list. He lay for almost a year, meeting the dark angel in the tunnel more than once. "It almost killed me," he states. Finally a little luck and a new heart gave him renewed hope of pursuing his beloved Mearns. This October saw him doing just that, gradually gaining strength, frequently accompanied by Dave.

Cobalt skies and a ten o'clock start found us chugging up gravel roads through steep passes. Insurmountable medical bills and continuing care and meds assure Gary will be nursing this pickup indefinitely. The banter starts immediately.

Dave, "I thought you got this fixed last week."

Gary, "I did."

Dave, "Then how come it's missing worse?"

Gary, "Guess they fixed the wrong part; they say it's electric."

Ted, "I don't think so. We'll dump in about five cans of dry gas IF we get back." (We did and it's fixed.)

Dave, "Tomorrow we take my truck."

The ten o'clock start is planned. "Mearns have manners," Gary maintains. They need time to gather in feeding coveys and to warm in the sun from the cold high desert nights.

Our dogs are a potpourri. I have Bobwhite specialist, Mildred, who will discover Mearns have a few new tricks. Gary has a seasoned veteran pointer who runs on three legs, and a green young pointer who lost half his tail. The best young dog Gary ever had succumbed after a thousand-dollar vet bill just when Gary got out of hospital. Quail can be hunted with flushing dogs as golf can be played with a broom. We leave Tweed home to comfort Dorothy and bring Arrow to exercise some weight off her. We decide to get this exercise bit over first thing and take off downhill into a swale behind the quartering Spaniel. Within half an hour she finds and flushes a twelve-bird covey. We all have shots, run down some singles and she makes the retrieves. We are back at the truck to let out the big dogs. Mildred disgraces herself almost immediately trying to pin a small covey of these strangely scented birds and flushes them out of range. Three hundred yards farther down the draw we get a marvelous point by the three-legged dog with staunch backs from the other two. Gary and Dave both shoot classic 410 doubles and are so quick that my 20-bore Holland and Holland—what they call "the cannon"—frequently tracks falling birds. During the next two hours we all connect, finding an unexpected seven conveys, very good for end of the season.

For Mearns I Yearn

To say this country is up and down is understatement. We constantly climb out of arroyos to the top of a straw-covered plateau, descending again down tree-covered precipices. At hunt's end, drinking iced Pacificos and passing my silver cup and flask filled with very old sherry, I am whipped. Though ever stoic, I detect a certain heaviness of step in Dave. Throughout, Gary and his new pump have performed admirably. He paces himself uphill, stopping requently. One of the odd quirks of his heart is it doesn't know when to speed up. It receives adrenalin that signals to step up the beat but has a built-in delay. Gary waits it out. On the flat he plods on at just the right pace for Mildred and his seasoned dog. I learn to slow up after a while. At hunt's end he is more rested than I. The unaccustomed altitude—over 7,000 feet—seems to favor a transplanted heart.

We bag just enough quail, but not too many. People gather at Dave's. Laurie and I prepare margaritas and a marinade of lime-juice, Tequila, Vermont maple syrup, olive oil and habanero sauce for the birds. Someone brought steaks so we prepare a "peep and turf" special. Others make salad, a schooled chef assembles all, a dessert materializes and as with all such perfect gatherings no one hurries; conversation, spirits and fine wine blend harmoniously in the comfortable surroundings of Dave's New England-style den and hearth. As I write this I review some notes made that evening that seemed brilliant at the time, but make no sense at all now.

During the week a filming crew arrives with a bizarre international project involving geese and ultra-lights. I spend a few moments with the head goose trainer. Before they are hatched the eggs are subjected to ultra-light noise. The Pavlovian gambit works and the mature geese fly in a V behind a piloted machine. The project is impressively funded and scheduled to air as a feature film.

Mearns may have manners, but they are damned unpredictable. In the next two days hunting similar and the same ground we are glad for the first day. The second day they simply evaporate and we find not one covey. Gary, who is expert on their habits, simply shrugs, after all these are Mearns. The last day is better; we locate three small groups. Mildred provides me a proud moment. Having figured out the scent cone these birds produce she nails several moving quail, circles and contains them from below. Now don't forget how to do this old girl, just in case we are invited back.

An interlude, a trip to Tucson to visit Lazlo, a fraternity house roommate. I have not seen him or Sue in forty years. A Hungarian freedom fighter student and world-class saber fencer, Lazlo came under the wire in 1956 with friends. They flipped a coin deciding between finishing their education in the States, or hunting kangaroos in Australia for bounty. Laz described the revolution as "hopeless but not serious." An advanced degree in petroleum geology provided a job in exploration with a major oil company from which he just retired. He has done very well, and in his still thick hunky accent he defends his golf game. "How many Hungarians do you see on the PGA tour?"

My return involves endless margaritas with a cast of characters including Bruce, the cowboy poet, golf on the Mexican border after which we walk across to dine elegantly. A week of pampering and we pack up, driving home a different way through hills and passes one would never expect in Texas.

A final evening at an old independent, the Slumber Motel, in Junction, Texas. The dogs and I share some kick butt barbeque at a picnic table in a soft late winter evening under so many stars the entire sky is the Milky Way.

Two days later my beloved Tweed IV will wander off at dusk on his last hunt into the prairie.

— 4 —

Hollowville, New York • January 2002

The Stonefly Sagas

The year: 1971— the onset of motor-home mania—self-propelled trailers made a lot of sense with the burgeoning Eisenhower Interstate system, cheap gas and insatiable American wanderlust. I was a sales rep for various ski-related products, covering northern New England ably assisted by my new wife. We had experimented with an odd fifth-wheel horror that we dragged protesting all the way attached to our tiny C5 Jeep. The rig scrubbed off tires every 5,000 miles. We saved on motels during the four-month selling season; our Spaniel, Tweed II could travel in comfort and we could use the thing for jaunts during the rest of the year. The concept had proven sound but the vehicle had not; we were ready to upgrade. I still have the sales agreement: purchase price $7,000, an Econoline chassis, underpowered by a Ford 301 with automatic transmission. The interior décor was Shasta manufacturing's idea of 1970s hip. The cupboards were psychedelic floral that resisted all efforts Kitty made to cover them with contact paper. They sloughed off like offending skin grafts, so she lived with the factory-installed epidermis. The design was brilliant. I look at modern units' layout within the seventeen-foot interior and there has been no improvement. It has a double bunk over the cab, open kitchen area, enclosed bath with shower and three more bunks in the rear that convert from the living/dining area. The propane furnace is central and has kept me alive, not necessarily comfy, at twenty below.

Stoner has outlasted our marriage by twenty-five years, requiring only routine maintenance, several transmission overhauls, an engine transplant of a rebuilt 351 Windsor, and a genius welder's complete replacement of the frame. Four years ago I drove it from Vermont to a field at Pondview Kennels, New York, where it served me until I relocated my home in central New York State this past summer. If I need to start it I can, and if I get too drunk to drive the forty minutes to my camp it still provides haven for me and up to four dogs.

The speedometer has spun so many times I have lost track, but it has at least 300,000 hard miles. I maintain that vehicles possess loyalty and integrity like people are supposed to. The lemons will break or strand you any chance they get. Determine this perfidy quick and sell them or they'll get you in the end. Stoner never failed me. Of course, we had our glitches and wrecks, but Stoner performed like your best horse. Thirteen round-trips to Montana, endless east to wests in New England and south to north in Canada provided ample opportunity for treachery. Never once.

How did Stoner get its name? Trout fishermen on western streams will tell of blanket hatches of giant stoneflies so dense at times as to blot out the sun. When these lumbering aerodynamically challenged bugs start dropping into the water every fish in the river becomes a taker. A "sofa pillow" imitation has to compete with hundreds of naturals in the feeding lanes, but if you can time your drift over a taking spot, my gosh, what a take and what a hog! Some wag compared Stoner's stately progress, particularly when dragging a boat trailer, to the stonefly's ponderous flight. The name stuck.

Though ever faithful, Stoner has always perched on the edge of disaster. Born in an era before steel shot and mandatory seatbelts, Stoner ferried countless numbers of fishing friends and gear between Vermont and the fabled western streams and rivers spanning a miraculous period of time from 1974 to 1993.

When young we pushed hard and took chances we didn't later on. We would think nothing of fishing until well after dark then driving all night through mountain passes to another river and different hatch.

The dumb alert light should have flashed and the siren whooped as we chugged up Wyoming's Ten Sleep Pass. One hundred degrees that day and one of the steepest grades up and down in the state. We had crossed it at night before and had discussed the possibility of going around. Fish greed had dulled our judgment. Stoner's brakes were never remotely adequate. It had only the brake system of a van, not the bloated body of a motor home almost double the weight. At the summit I came to a near stop and down-shifted to low. The first couple of miles were fine. I feathered the brakes and cheated over the line on corners. Gradually the smell of burning linings wafted into the cab. I had planned on stopping in several pull-offs on the way down, but there weren't any in time to prevent meltdown. There was plenty of pedal, but the entire system had heated to the point where there was no friction between the shoes and drums. We were in fact heading for freefall with at least eight miles of bottomless canyons and hairpins ahead. I had alerted my three companions of our impending doom and started looking for a bailout. A truck run-out sign appeared and I decided on this route. We shot around a hairpin and there it was — a side road up the mountainside, a quarter mile of pea gravel. "Hang on, this is going to be rough!" I yelled. These run-outs are numerous throughout the West and on a few eastern slopes. They are designed as a last fail-safe for fully loaded runaway eighteen-wheelers headed for oblivion. Not for little single wheel contraptions with smoking brakes. We hit the gravel, and there was a second of fishtailing that could have rolled us. Then a very quick stop. Gear and bodies flew everywhere inside the thing. When the dust cleared the interior looked like an implosion at a surplus store. I took human inventory; both Peters were shaken but whole. Tony was still lying unphased on the back bunk. "Are we there yet?" he asked. Tony had been in Vietnam as an adviser in the early phases of the conflict. A price paid for joining ROTC at Dartmouth. In the aftermath of a successful ambush the VC had walked through prodding the few survivors of Tony's patrol with feet and bayonets and dispatching the ones that moved. Tony fooled them either because he was unconscious from a mortar round, or able to withstand the prodding. In any case, a simple off-road experience in Stoner was not even worthy of serious thought. Somewhere there is a photo from 1978 of the four of us posed outside a forlorn Stoner mired up to the hubs in pea gravel. We employed a wrecker to haul us down. We rented a bay to correct the only damage—gravel crammed through any possible opening into the wheels. All four wheels had to be removed from the spindles and the stones dug out. Conveniently located across the street was a saloon that provided frequent breaks from our labors. One of the local patrons told of his descent down Ten Sleep Pass driving a Coors truck. He lost his brakes but decided to go for it. "By the time I hit the last turn I was going over seventy. I almost made it, but instead she flipped, beer kegs everywhere. One bounced through the front of a house. As quick as I could get to a phone I called the distributor. 'I quit!' Since then

The Stonefly Sagas

I've been a wreck. I can't haul beer anymore; I just sit here and drank (drink) it."

Considering the number of miles, the tough use and laughable design flaws, Stoner had very few wrecks. It doesn't even have dual wheels in the back. We coaxed it miles, through brush-clogged ranch roads along the North Platte and the Henry's Fork. Places you wouldn't even take a rental car. It is a surprisingly good snow vehicle. Only one incident resulted in an entire side torn off. While waiting at a light in St. Johnsbury, Vermont, a drunk in a pickup swerved into us exposing and scrambling both full propane tanks. The drunk kept going either to escape or possibly unaware he had hit anything.

We used to leave Vermont, four of us, and drive straight through, stopping only for gas and increasing amounts of oil as Stoner seasoned. The trip and finances were highly structured. Each of us put in the same amount of money when needed. One was banker. We drove two-hour shifts, no more no less, in rotation. This allowed six hours off for looking out the window, tying flies, reading, napping. One trip I tied knots, learning an entire system developed by Dupont Stren for any attachment of fishing line based on a circle. Cribbage scores were carried over year to year. I was alone in my enjoyment of watching the Midwest as seen from I-80 glide by, particularly the neat little homesteads in Iowa with their freshly painted outbuildings. Places you would love to be invited for Thanksgiving.

Driving Stoner well was not automatic. Its mass relative to the small single wheels made for big corrections with very skittish steering every time a semi whooshed by. My rule was to maintain 62 MPH to save gas and wear on the vehicle. For some reason we kept accurate records of mileage on each tank of gas. Of course other drivers would wait for me to crash, and then push up to 70. No matter what we did we averaged 10 MPG.

For extended fishing two was ideal, three all right and four a crowd. Two had to sleep juxtaposed feet to head in the top bunk. Gear paranoia was punctuated by plaintive bleating: "Has anyone seen my . . . grey sock . . . fly box . . . camera lens . . . toothbrush . . . cap? Most always the missing item showed up in a few days. It was amazing how well we all got along over the years without serious arguments or violence. In good weather we surrounded Stoner with campfires, lanterns, drying racks for clothes and waders. We were pros.

I was very poor at the time, squeaking out an existence teaching skiing in winter, and as a ski sales rep and tennis teacher the rest of the year. I remember stopping on the way out of town in Burlington to borrow $500 from a lady friend so I could make the trip. Pooling funds, it was remarkable how well we lived for extended periods and enjoyed spectacular fishing with very little money. Stoner was the key.

Along the way Stonefly acquired a soul mate. We fastened an ancient moped on the front, which served as our transfer vehicle between floats. I once rode, pushed and carried it seventy miles on ranch roads along Montana's Smith River. This vehicle was never named but still runs and the speedometer is broken at over five thousand miles; this must be a record of some kind.

As has been suggested, these chronicles could easily be a book, so I'll cover all in a few short vignettes. Matt actually got Stoner's only speeding ticket in Hailey, Idaho. I had been guiding his sons for the summer from one blue-ribbon river to another with him joining us on several occasions. The speed limit he broke was 30 MPH and I argued with the cop that it was Stoner's top speed. It was in rough shape. I nursed it home in 110-degree drought conditions, getting fifty miles to the quart of oil. When I got back Matt installed a 351 Windsor engine, which even provided a passing gear.

We dropped the gas tank on the way home from a goose hunt. Stonefly continued to go down the highway dragging it. The only reason we stopped before incineration was that J.D. saw the sparks flying out the back through his side mirror.

For several years during the months of August and September Stonefly went to the Rhode Island shore. My fishing partner, Bill, and I were ski reps in the late seventies during the snow drought. I watched my cross-country ski sales deteriorate to nothing. Bill owned a classic twenty-two foot Aquasport adequately propelled. He had cleverly obtained a commercial saltwater fishing license. These were times of abundant bluefish and sea trout. Though we spurned trolling and wire line I am not proud of the fact that we would sell one thousand pounds of fish taken by plugging and even fly rods on occasion. The co-op at the dock in Galilee paid twenty cents a pound heads on and cleaned. I then had a restaurant route on the way back to Vermont through fish-starved inland New England. I sold the blues for $1 a pound and sometimes added to the total by bootlegging lobsters.

Stoner parked free in the marina; we supplied the owner's grandchildren with free ski equipment and served as the mother ship. We would take the wet trip to Block Island, where we would fish for two or three days. I stashed an old and unreliable wagon in the airport parking lot. When it ran it got us around the seven-mile island and to the bars. In winter it took me around the deserted place to surprisingly well-populated pheasant covert. We slept in the wagon and used the men's room in the airport. No one cared. Sometimes if the catch was plentiful we would stay in an old sailor's hotel we named "The Empty Arms."

Now when I struggle for a couple of blues to grill I think back to those days of excess. At any rate we certainly found uses for the little money we earned fishing.

Despite brake failures, breakdowns, poor maintenance, dragging gas tanks, no one was ever injured in or by Stoner with one exception, which happened recently. After an infusion of single malt—I should never drink it—I fell out of the top bunk landing liver first on the metal corner of the stove. My entire side bruised black and a swelling the size of a lemon appeared in the location of my liver. The cure was to let it disperse over several months. Doctors have sedulously sought to kill me with their treatments, so I don't go to them. It went away and obviously my liver survived to continue my assault on it.

Stoner came close to expiring when I left it with a young angler to drive home from Wyoming, because I had a real job for a change at *Outdoor Life* in New York city with a desk requiring me to fly back to. Against all odds, twenty years old and tired, Bullet made it home in Stoner alone without incident. The unnamed moped was attached to the rear bumper by yellow braided rope. He never checked the knots or the rope and arrived in my driveway in Vermont with the moped secured by one thin strand of the original eight. The other seven had worn through. I still have nightmares of the moped bouncing down the Interstate through the windshield of a family of four.

Stoner was not a good vehicle to cross the border to Canada. Over the years it acquired hundreds of stickers, many political in nature and NRA inspired. In handgun-banned Canada the artistic rendering of a revolver pointed at the customs booth with the appropriate slogan would raise a few official eyebrows. We avoided the border as often as possible in Stoner, particularly after an eager vehicle- and strip-search on the way into Nova Scotia. The chubby and sweating little agent went into every potential cachet for over an hour. He could have found almost anything in there. Numerous people of all ages had been passengers throughout the freewheeling seventies and eighties. Triumphantly he pulled a film canister from behind a cushion. I paled. It was empty.

Stonefly's last trip West was one of the best. I was working for a publishing company in Minnesota. Graham was working for me. We lost power steering on the way to Minneapolis and wrestled it there for a meeting and had it repaired. We continued west and for a month, fished all my favorite spots and a few new ones. The fishing was phenomenal but the entire trip was a mechanical nightmare. Stoner kept stopping dead. We replaced fuel pumps, carbs, and every filter to no avail. It would run fine until it decided not to. Stoner was telling me something and I laid my love affair with western trout to rest. I kid myself every now and then that I will fire it up for one last cross-county jaunt, but we are both too old. It sits with all tires inflated, which differentiates it from a derelict. When it gets warmer I will take my jumper cables, wrenches and a strong battery and take bets that I can't take it for a spin.

— 5 —

Cape Breton Island • Late July 2000

Bathtubs on Anticosti Island

The weather has broken! It's pouring rain with winds from the east. It looks like at least a two-dayer, and to a salmon fisherman this means those eager spawners waiting in the gulf will streak up river.

The fishing has been terrible of late—day after day of hot beach weather has lowered the salmon pools and the water temperature is approaching the dangerous seventy-degree mark, which is tough on fish. I no longer fish in these conditions. I am not as mad at the salmon as I used to be. The poor oxygen-deprived fish lie on the bottom like somnolent toads, and if you do happen to hook one and release it there is strong research that indicates an exhausted fish in warm water has diminished hopes of survival. I must say I see few fish belly-up floating back to sea, so this could be exaggerated. I little fault visitors with their guides pounding these pools; what choice do they have? I do greatly fault obsessed locals who hook the same fish multiple times. It isn't necessary or fair. Sometimes I will fish the tidal pools in a hot spell, and occasionally hook a bright salmon that doesn't know there has been no fresh water for a month. That fish released is a good candidate for survival, at least until some human cormorant hooks or snags him in knee-deep water in an upper pool.

Ten years ago at Anticosti Island on a minor river (not the Jupiter) I was the unwilling participant in the most severe low-water conditions I ever hope to see. Over one hundred fish were trapped in a bathtub pool forty yards long and twenty wide warmed by a blazing sun. In a river that size it could have been a large percentage of the run. There was no navigable water above or below. Four of us were committed for seven days, and these were the only fish in the river. In other trips on a different river I have been saved from abject boredom and alcohol poisoning by a voracious sea trout run. This river did not have a run of them, so these super-stressed salmon were it. This was in the time of a two-fish daily limit, which everyone killed.

We split up, and my partner and I went down to the estuary, which was choked with weeds that first morning. The other two went upriver, returning with three grilse and a salmon from the bath tub by nine A.M.

The tone was set for the week, which just got brighter and hotter, with less water running into the pool from the little spate river. By the week's end I had counted and even named the big salmon that remained stressed and on station. Sadly, an overhanging spruce was decorated for Christmas with numerous flies and harbored several illegal spinning lures from an earlier party. The best hope was first fly on the pool early in the morning (no surprise). We shamelessly flogged the water throughout the day and every now and then a fish would break out of the pod and take. I was particularly interested in the effect false casting had on them. They absolutely panicked if lined, probably a memory of being small and vulnerable to avian assault. To this day I keep false casting to a bare minimum, even with dries.

After we departed I was delighted to learn a major storm came through to save these brave creatures from certain death.

This was not my last trip to this strange and beautiful island. Over one hundred miles long, its pinewoods teem with wildlife, including whitetails whose bodies have shrunk but still support magnificent racks. Foxes and otters come right up to you while you are fishing. Jupiter's deep aquamarine pools make it one of the spectacularly beautiful salmon rivers in the world. Now managed by the Quebec government, it has a checkered past. At one point it was purchased by a peculiar Frenchman (from France) whose family made its fortune in chocolate. The tiny settlement, Port Menier, is named for him and was dominated by his Baroque mansion until fire destroyed it. He planned a Utopian society and began the experiment by populating the island with exotic game. It is rumored that the quarries were at times human and consumed. A recalcitrant, Angus MacDonald, after whom a river was named, refused to pay homage and is buried with an appropriate stone at the site of his homestead. I had a long chat with him one night and found this dedicated francophobe to be reasonable in every respect. I even scribed a mock epic in the styles of Joseph Conrad and H.P. Lovecraft, which I delivered by candlelight at our traditional banquet. Into the story was weaved a cast of demons from the island's past and present.

We tried another river, and I joined the group twice more with modest luck, but never with sufficient water. I either had to move to Anticosti, which took on increasingly weird aspects for me, or move on, which I did.

— 6 —

WATERBURY, VERMONT • NOVEMBER 1978

The Twilight Season

This story was written by my hunting buddy Peter Miller and first appeared in *Sports Afield* in 1978. He plans to have carved on his tombstone I WOULD RATHER BE WOODCOCK HUNTING.

My friend Ross is a traditionalist; he likes to hang the past into the present. For instance, bird season always commences with breakfast at his house, a breakfast of salted codfish cakes, the type that come in those thin, wooden boxes from Nova Scotia. God only knows why codfish cakes should mark the first day of the woodcock season.

"Well, Miller," Ted will say, year after year, with a brilliant smile lighting up his red face, as I walk in, suited for the occasion with frazzled canvas pants, my hunting vest, and a white plastic whistle hung around my neck with a piece of clothesline, "Here we are again. I hope that no good dog of yours will do something decent today."

My Brittany, Parker, has hustled over to Tweed's dish and is gulping down his meal. Ted's dog, a Springer, is a fussy eater, and needs to have meat mixed in with kibble.

"Oh, shut up," Ted retorts. "Tweed is ten times the dog Parker ever will be. Eat your codfish cakes!"

"God, they stink to high heaven!" But they taste better than they smell. Even the eggs are good, one thing Ted can't cook well.

It is the official beginning of fall, and in Vermont, there is no finer season for color, the fragrance of the woods, released when the sun melts the frost, the softness of morning fog burying the valleys, the clarity of the air, and the absolute joy of hunting birds with an old friend and two old reliable dogs.

Tweed is going on fourteen. Skinny and frail, but looking younger than his age, he sees Ted take the over-and-under out of the gun rack. Suddenly the Springer loses a dozen years. So does Parker. A little more than a year younger than Tweed, she was once more orange than white with good ticking over her muzzle, but now she is grizzled and overweight. She breathes heavily, and her joints are also stiff, but she too scents the excitement of opening day. Both have lived so long for the simple pleasure of hunting through the fall.

Parker and Tweed never liked each other, not since they first hunted together ten years ago. Parker, a female and quite a femme fatale in her heyday, never could quite stomach Tweed, who is a bit effeminate, which has won him the nickname of Mildred. Tweed would sniff up Parker; Parker would growl and Tweed would stiff leg it out of range. Still, they learned to accommodate each other, in the house, in the car, and in the field. Who would ever think you could hunt a pointer and flusher together? Well, you really can't when they're young. You trade one off on the other. But when they are a little older it works out fine.

Both dogs live at home and have the run or our houses; they live our lives. They have been by our side during financial disaster, divorce, a number of affairs, some very drunken evenings, and some very good times.

"Look at it this way, Miller," Ted said to me ten years ago after my marriage disintegrated and he loaded me and the remnants of my life into his pickup, the Easter Pig, and moved me from my house to an apartment, "you have your fishing rod, your shotgun and your dog. What else do you need?"

A few years later, when Ted when through the same treatment, I fed him back the same advice. If our two dogs were writers, they could publish a saga of the various stages of American marriage, and the emasculating effects of the American divorce, and follow it up with some rousing stories about bachelorhood. In a way, our two dogs, good old Park and Tweed, remained the only stability during this transitional period.

It is as traditional for us to hunt the potato field as it is to eat codfish cakes for breakfast. The cover is about twenty acres bounded on the south by a lake and marsh. The river that sustains the lake cleaves the cover from a wooded hillside. To the north is the potato field, which in some years becomes a cornfield. To the west is a small lagoon, then trees and mountains. The cover is rich, and so is the soil, judging from the number of woodcock that summer there, and the flight birds that settle in sporadically during the season, night visitors, known only to us and our dogs. The cover also holds partridge, who feed on the alders, poplars and wild grapes that grow thickly in two sections. Occasionally we see a deer sneak through the woods in front of us. Beaver have cut small waterways and made trails. They have done much to keep the cover from growing over and turning fallow. So have the spring floods that will scour a portion of the cover, leaving behind a new layer of topsoil.

There is an old road that goes partially into the cover and then becomes a tractor trail. It is about a half-mile long, and because it seems to lead nowhere but to a plowed potato field, few hunters know about it. Only once did I see a trespasser in there, an old man that I saw from the distance, with hip boots and shotgun in hand, crossing the stream with a black-and-white Setter. He hid from me as I hid from him, and I have the sneaking suspicion that Ted and I have shared this cover with him for years. We usually hit the potato field no more than three or four times a season, and maintain a minimum harvest so the native woodcock will return and the partridge will produce another year.

I found the cover over a dozen years ago, before I had a dog. The potato field was the first cover I took Parker to hunt in. I had expected little from Parker, for although I had trained her on all the commands, the young pup had refused to point at the grouse wing I had. Yet on the first day I hunted her, the first day of the season, she pointed. I was so surprised I missed twice on a rising woodcock. Then she pointed throughout the potato field, down the gully near the beaver canal, on the ridge between the thin alder cover and the marsh, in the poplars, where there always is a bird. I shot my limit that first day over Parker, hugged her, kissed her, and readily forgave her for not retrieving the birds. She would find them, worry them, but not retrieve.

That first day Parker and I became a very close team and confidants in a secret life too. My home at the time was a battlefield, heavily infiltrated by the enemy. Skirmishes were continual, and Parker and I, the brunt of these attacks, found relief, and about the only joy, in the woods.

Later, when Ted and I became friends, and we learned to trust one another enough to divulge to each other our favorite woodcock coverts, and to hunt with each other safely and with confidence, we worked the birds, sometimes with Tweed, a headstrong pup, and sometimes with Parker. Tweed delighted in busting out birds ahead of us. Parker was not too bad, at times, but did her share of bumping them and hunting out the range. Ted would call his dog in and scream at him a while, while I gnashed my teeth, then Parker would bump birds, or vanish beyond whistle range, and Ted would say, "It certainly isn't Parker's day, is it?"

And I would gnash my teeth again. When I would miss an easy shot, blowing out shot from both barrels of my Parker before I could even aim, Ted would stand there, screaming,

"Miller, how could you?" as we both watched the bird curve around an alder and wing it down the river to the other bank.

Yet we had our good moments in the potato field and in other covers through the years. We hit a number of partridge in 1969, when the potato field was no more than a jungle; the cover was so thick, we thought we missed, but Tweed had retrieved three of them.

We hunted over some classic points. We would analyze the bird's escape route and then, with Parker steady, head down, one of us crept in, the other holding outside, hoping to have a shot. One of us usually brought down a bird. We never went home empty-handed, and roasted woodcock, with trail on toast, became one of the delights of October.

Now the dogs are old, their combined life span, in our age, was 174 years. Ted and I had moved on a bit too. We had survived our marriages to become hardened bachelors and learned to look at anything but hunting and fishing with a slightly cynical eye. Our infirmities were beginning to show. My hip, an old football injury, bothered me on cold days, and my knees pained me when we hunted hillside covers. Ted moved slower, and his hearing in one ear was quite dull. It took longer for both of us to recover from celebrating the delights of hunting the night before.

But the dogs were much worse off than us. Tweed was almost totally deaf and would hunt only by scent and sight. His ticker was so decrepit that two digitalis pills kept him moving. Pain killers eased his arthritis. Parker in this twilight season had gone stone deaf. She couldn't hear my whistle. Her arthritis was also so bad that at times I would have to carry her into the car and up the stairs at home. Her eyes were glazing over with cataracts and her lungs sounded bad; she still hunted with elan, but she wheezed like a steam locomotive.

Ted and I discussed this before the season.

"Well, Christ, Miller, both these dogs live for hunting. They'd die quicker if we didn't hunt them, and what better way for them to go then in the field? I'd just as soon go that way myself. How would you like to be kept home and petted while your dog went hunting?"

"Depends on who does the petting," I retorted, but we both knew we would hunt our dogs until they couldn't walk, and our dogs would appreciate us for it.

Neither of us would consider acquiring a younger dog. That would cause heartbreak, and I know it would kill Parker. She didn't like young dogs at all, and to see another dog invade her home would be like divorcing and remarrying another woman and living with both in the same house.

Ted and I worked our dogs before the season. Ted would jog a couple of miles with his dog. I would sniff around new covers, looking for birds, and give Parker and myself a workout. The first days my dog was breathing so heavily we had to stop and rest, and I feared old Park would need to be carried home. Day by day she improved, and I mixed meat and boiled egg in her kibble, and stuck in a vitamin pill for dessert. On a trip to New York she even had an electrocardiogram, and she appeared, to this city doctor, to be in superb shape.

It was our tenth opening day spent in the potato field with Tweed and Parker. We parked our car in the woods so nobody would see it, belled our dogs and unsheathed our guns. The same old giddy feeling crept over me as the dogs grew nervous and raring to go, the same excitement I felt when I was six and my father was taking me and his Setter, Lady, out for the opening day. I was all lightness and smiles inside. I hefted my Parker 16. Smooth, fast, filled with grace, I would be deadly.

When the dogs were young we would hunt one or the other. Later, they could hunt together, Tweed quartering to the right, my dog to the left. Occasionally, Parker would go on point, Ted would order Tweed to hold, and we would flush and shoot the bird with Tweed doing the fetching. Both dogs, to tell the truth, weren't much good at all until they had passed their fifth birthday. Parker came into her prime when she was six and didn't slow down until she was ten. She was always a slow hunter and so am I, and that is why we would account for thirty woodcock every season for dinners through Christmas.

When Parker turned nine, arthritis was setting into her hindquarters and her hearing, when I blew the whistle, wasn't the best. Tweed, on the other hand, would have been dead from a heart attack at ten if it wasn't for the double dose of digitalis pills. His hearing started to go when he was eleven.

Now both of our dogs couldn't hear a bloody thing, but we still carried whistles around our necks due to tradition, and sometimes to blow out of frustration.

"Hunt 'em up!" I would say to the dogs, and Ted and I invaded the cover, the dogs running in front. They didn't hear the command, they just did what comes naturally.

We had learned, hunting with our old dogs, that the role was reversed. As pups, the young dogs hunted wildly, and slowly we trained them to hunt for us. Now we hunted for our dogs. They would go their way, and we would follow. Whistles wouldn't help to bring them in. Parker would jump up to look for me, and I waved my hand quite a bit. When she was close enough so the cataracts weren't bothering her vision, I could direct her with hand signals. If she wandered off too far, she would cut a circle, find my scent, and hone in on me. Tweed would do the same. At first, Ted and I did a bit of cussing, but we learned to relax about it. Our old dogs hunted more efficiently, for they knew instinctively they didn't have the strength. They became more thorough in chasing up birds, and because they worked closer, we had more shots. We learned to pace ourselves to our dog's pace, and every so often we would rest, enjoy the beauty of the woods, savor the wood's aroma as our dogs lay around us, panting and slowly regaining their strength. Then off again. We would hunt several hours, relax, and hunt again. On longer days we would round robin the dogs, leaving one in the car as we hunted the other and moved from cover to cover.

We were resting in the potato field cover near the stream after I had downed two woodcock over points and Ted had brought one down in a flush. It had taken me longer than usual to find the birds; the cover was thick and Tweed was losing his nose. Parker even found one. Ted was reminiscing about hunting with geriatric dogs.

"You know," he told me, mopping his brow and holding his red crusher hat to fan his face. It was a warm day after the sun burned off the fog. "I was trained to hunt by an old dog. He belonged to a friend of my father's, and was called Nod. If I missed, the dog went straight home.

Our dogs were in charge as we moved upstream to the wild grape tangle. Parker started to make scent, moving forward, her tail pumping, head low. I knew it was a partridge. Tweed was working downwind, out of sight.

"Parker's on a grouse," I yelled, and ran forward as the grouse flushed. Instead of flying over the stream the bird flew along the bank.

"Overhead!" I screamed after I shot twice and missed and damned myself for shooting too fast. Parker gave me one of those looks. We moved to the riverbank and worked downstream to where we thought the bird had landed. Tweed started his scent dance, Ted warned me and the bird flew out of thick alders and across the stream. We both shot. A puff of feathers immobilized itself behind the bird, then drifted downstream as the bird fell thirty yards away into the stream near the far bank.

"Fetch!" Ted commanded Tweed. Tweed went two steps in the water, came out and gave his master a look as if to say, "Not on your life, buddy." Parker wouldn't even think of going in the stream and both headed back to the alders, expecting us to follow.

"Well, Miller, I guess we are the retrievers," and we headed in the stream, going over our boots. The partidge was caught in a swirl next to a rock, and I went down to retrieve it. The dogs looked on from the other shore. Then Parker swam across. Tweed followed, but the current carried him down and the dog frantically treaded water.

"He's in trouble!" yelled Ted, and handed me his gun as he scrambled down the bank. He slipped and landed in the stream up to his neck and gave me a look that was about the same as

Tweed was wearing—"Help!" Ted takes to water like a pussy cat. He grabbed Tweed and the two of them, soaked like dishrags, made it to shore. I was on my knees, chocking with laughter as Parker sat beside me.

Water was dripping off Ted's nose, and I could hear it gurgle and slosh in his hunting vest.

"What's so goddamned funny?" We walked upstream to find a crossing, carried the dogs across and left for home.

We dried the dogs off, changed our clothes and finished the potato field cover in the afternoon. Parker made a staunch point, head down, not moving a muscle. Quiet filled the vacuum this dog and I and woodcock made; I heard myself breathing, flexed my muscles and moved in, balancing on both feet, slightly swinging, scanning with my eyes unfocused, left and right, waiting for the bird to flush. Suddenly it was up, moving fast. For some reason, this season's woodcock did not tower, they shot up in a hurry. The gun moved up in that unconscious motion I had learned through the years and the bird was down.

Parker had not budged. She was still on point, head down. I walked up, retrieved the bird, brought it back and dropped it in front of her. She broke then, mouthed the bird once and gave me a look of pride and satisfaction that we had both done our job. She had not heard my shot, nor had she seen the bird flush, nor had she seen me retrieve the bird. I knew then, and it made me shiver a bit, that we were perhaps partaking in our last season.

Tweed scouted up another woodcock for Ted, and then Tweed and Parker vanished. We could not hear the bells, and we began scouting, each going in a different direction. I thought Parker might be on point and kept ducking down, looking around. Ten minutes later I found her, lying down, her front paws crossed as she does at home sometimes, giving me that where-have-you-been look.

"Park, whatcha doing there? Come on," but Parker remained quiet, taking it easy. Suddenly I understood. The woodcock flushed and moved to the right, scrambling around a poplar. I was on it, thank God, and the bird was down. Parker found it, mouthed it, gave me a look as if to say "about time," then moved on.

In the lazy warmth of the afternoon we lifted Tweed and Park into the back of the station wagon and drove home. It was a good opening for the first day of the season with two geriatric, stone-deaf dogs and their over-the-hill hunters. We flushed eight woodcock. Parker pointed five and I shot four. Ted brought down two over Tweed, and we shared one partridge. A typical opening day in the potato field. That night we celebrated with a woodcock meal for two lady friends. Our dog friends were zonked out, not moving.

The fall of '77 was a good season. The leaves rattled off the trees early in October as the winds scrubbed the coverts and opened up the shooting. Although the flights did not appear, we found singles and doubles of woodcock, and the most partridge in a decade. Many times I hunted only with Parker in covers known by names that mean something special to the two of us— the Iron Bridge Cover, the Cows That Scared Parker—Cover, the Love Cover, Where I Got the Double Cover—patches of alders and poplars scattered throughout Vermont, worthless pieces of wet land and small brooks and hillside overgrown mowings of value only to a dog such as Parker and a hunter like me.

It was a dark wet day late in October, but I had time to hunt and the scent should be good so I drove Parker to the Swimming Hole Cover, named because there is a curve in the brook that is deep and rock edged. A willow leans over the hole and a swinging rope hangs from a branch. Occasionally, in the fall, Parker and I will scare a trout that darts upstream, a dark arrow in a narrow stream. The brook is surrounded by alders that are heavily fertilized by woodcock and the grass clipped by cows. Higher up are apple trees, more alders and thick second-growth hardwoods. I hit a flight in there once, with Park, and came out with a limit. We were again looking for it.

The stream meanders in a serpentine fashion, so you must cross it several times. We found no birds in the first two patches along the stream, not even chalk, so I decided to move to the higher cover. Parker was working my right, and I expected her to move up the hill after I crossed. She didn't show, and I walked back to the stream, thinking she was on point.

I spotted her, downstream, stretched out, lifeless, the water streaming over her. "My God," I muttered, dropped my Parker, ran into the water and dragged her out to the bank, grassy and clean where the heifers had browsed. I opened her mouth, pulled the tongue and began beating on her chest. But she hadn't drowned, she had just died. She was gone. I lay there on the ground, my two hands on her, the water soaking her, and rested my head on her flank. "Oh God, Parker," I whispered. "Park, oh Park."

I carried her about a half-mile to the car and took her home. In the old bathtub I washed the dirt and gravel from her. She looked so old, so different. I put her in a plastic sack, took the shovel out of the garage, and drove up to the potato field.

In the corner we always hunted first, and where there was always a bird, and only about one hundred yards from where she pointed her first woodcock, twelve years ago, I buried her with her collar, the bell I used that was hung on a leather ski strap I had cut down, and the white plastic whistle, tied to the old piece of soft clothesline. I marked the grave with a few bricks then squatted down. There was a slight wind blowing and it was damp, a hunter's type of damp, good scent weather. A song bird fluttered

The Twilight Season

overhead, stopped on a branch, and looked us over. Branches from the alders moved softly in the wind. There was still a touch of color in the range on the other side of the potato field, but most of the leaves were down, and the colors were gray and mauve, the early colors of November. That evening Ted came over and we mournfully drank our way through the night.

— 7 —

HOLLOWVILLE, NEW YORK • MARCH 2002

Chester Weir(d)

About thirty miles down the Henry's Fork from the famed Railroad Ranch but light years away from that esoteric trout shrine is Chester Weir. You have to buy an Idaho license to fish there. "The Ranch" is a bastion for purists fishing for huge trout with small flies and tackle and the revered green drake hatch and lesser known brown drake. Six X leader is the norm and a Social Register of anglers return every year to walk in and flail these hallowed riffles and pools. I was never comfortable there, though I did fool a couple of outsized rainbows in the twenty-eight inch range.

Downriver you are more likely to find local spin fishermen using spoons and bait rather than bluebloods casting thorax-tied size 22 trichos. The aspect upriver is green and alpine, the sharp drop to Chester ends in semi arid ranchland, heavily irrigated. To get to the Weir involves ninety-degree angle turns over irrigation ditches on five miles of rough ranch road, no mean feat in a motor home towing a canoe trailer. This is not park land, but privately owned by a rancher who must like fishermen. How Peter R. ever found this spot was never disclosed. A poor cousin to the

Chester Weir(d)

Henry's Fork joins just above the dam. It has a name that I have forgotten; I fished it once for its small, foot-long hybrid rainbows. In the East it would be blue ribbon but not out there. I have a 1980 photo still taped on the refrigerator in Stonefly, my revered camper, of Matt F. and son Peter sharing with me a breakfast beer in this magical spot. The banks are green, the current flows slow but sure toward the dam. Several angry cattle are in residence. Fifteen-year-old Peter had unsuccessfully attempted to topple them the night before while they slept. Not much in the way of fishing goes on during the day at the Weir. After the third visit I didn't bother, opting for camp, sunbathing and swimming in the deep pool at the junction of the two rivers. Depending on the flow the more rapid Henry's Fork does funny things to the bow of a canoe as you paddle across sluggish deadwater into its current. The pervasive sage aroma is stronger here than any other place in the West I have visited. There are daytime options for the fanatical. Go across and paddle up the far shore as far as you can go; beach the canoe where the big riffle ends. Fish that riffle with a size 14 Hornberg just under the surface and sometimes take those little sixteen inchers until your arms tire.

Knowing what the evening holds in store, why tire yourself? I developed a ritual approach: several stiff drinks in a camp chair, a snack and cocking my ears for the first twilight splash. This heralded the movement of the caddis moths from the willows to the river. "All right, boys, man the boats and let's go!" Across the point dividing the two rivers the acrobatics were in progress. Caddis out to drink or lay their eggs, spent mayflies on a one-way to the dam. Several nocturnal hatches enrich the stew and here are four frantic anglers gibbering and casting to old raises. The big fish an enigma. Whether they were bottom feeders which came up for the nightly banquet or whether they followed the spinner fall down to the Weir we never determined. What we did determine was we could not catch them. Sure we took the odd twenty-incher, but the true hogs of Chester Weir never felt the hook.

As I think back, I don't believe there were as many true hogs as there appeared, but the action was so fraught with adrenaline that the few whales that did come up among the hundreds of simultaneous raises seemed like more. Of course when one of these leviathans sounded, you could not help casting to where it had been. In a still pool fish will adapt a circular cruising pattern, but no pattern or logic prevailed here.

A new magazine job enabled Graham H. and me to take back-to-back extended trips in Stonefly in the early '90s. I was no longer on a payroll but on commission and Graham was working for me. The excellent publisher who hired us was Minnesota-based, which allowed us to stop on the way out and back. Otherwise we had no constraints so long as the work got done.

Needless to say Chester was on the must-visit list; I even bought the cheapest inflatable and electric motor from Bass Pro, for the Weir is not fished from shore. The craft came with a leak, which required frequent hand pumping while afloat. The tiny electric was not quite powerful enough to get as far upriver as we would have liked, but strong enough to keep us from going over the dam at the end of a slow drift.

The first year was a disappointment. For two days the hatches never really happened. It was boiling hot. We took the odd fish but never experienced the evening feeding frenzy. We decided to wait one more evening and leave early to head north to cooler water. It was almost dark when I heard the first volley of splashes signaling that the caddis had lifted out of the bushes.

"Where's the boat?"

"I let the air out and packed it up like you told me to half an hour ago."

I knew that by the time we got operational the raise would be a memory. I don't remember giving that order and the discussion of whether I did or didn't was quite heated over the next week.

The next year found us there at about the same time with two days to invest. The water temperature was ten degrees cooler. The first evening was a sad duplicate of the past trip. The second day in broad daylight it started. The splashes woke me from an afternoon siesta. It was a circus. My partner got the "yips" setting the hook and breaking off an endless number of eighteen-inch fish. Added to his woes was the fact that the leak had become more pronounced over the year. I had patched and tested it in the half-hearted manner you repair objects you truly despise.

Between breaking off trout and working the hand pump it was time for a rest at the bottom of the drift. I threw over our brake caliper anchor. Ashore two Hispanics were casting bait and enveloped in a cloud of blue narcotic smoke. I was trailing a small Adams probably slightly under the surface and trying to light a Sweet cigar when the Rainbow of my dreams took. I remember at least four mighty leaps and then the trout pulled us around at will, oftimes fairly close to the dam. Graham had switched to a paddle and we were not in danger. I brought this beauty along side—it must have been thirty inches in length—reached down and flicked the fly loose. The hombres on shore howled obscenities in disbelief. I guess they felt if I didn't want it I could have at least conked it on the head and given it to them.

From that point on I am not as trout-crazed as I once had been. I like the occasional trophy like anyone else, but I no longer hunger.

Later on I received the sad news of the passing of Peter R.'s father. I sent the following telegram:

"Peter, just got the news and sorry I was not in the East for the services. But I did finally take one of the hogs of Chester Weir(d)."

— 8 —

Moscow, Vermont • April 2000

The Cruelest Month and Falling In

That particular time in northern New England known as mud season has arrived. There is a misconception that there is no real spring in Vermont; just "eight months of winter and four months of damn poor sleddin.'" Most years this isn't true. A glorious summer is heralded by a fecund albeit brief spring, but this sure isn't it.

The mud itself is a product of three factors: frost melting out of the ground, snowmelt and copious rain. This year all the factors are star-crossed, hence lots of mud. Of course, decades ago when most of the roads were unpaved and scrapers were in their infancy, mud could be legendary. Prior to Interstates a six-mile section of the major north-south Route 100 was at times impassable to the hordes of skiers going north to enjoy the last corn snow. One entrepreneurial ski instructor used to wait in the bar I owned for tourists to get stuck in the lot. It would cost $10 for him to get off his stool to tow them out with his 4-wheel-drive. Some nights he did very well indeed, even after his cut to the management. Small towns were cut off; one of them to this day is named Mud City.

There is even mud humor: The proprietor of Ernest Shigley's Barber Shop, Morgue and General Store is sitting on the porch of his establishment, rocking in the sun. He spies his old friend Marvin Magoon coming down Main Street with only his head and hat visible above the sea of mud.

"Mornin' Ernest."

"Mornin' Marvin. Mud's kinda deep ain't it."

"Oh, I'll be fine, Ernest, so long as I have my horse under me."

And there is little to do. There is spring skiing for some, and it is frequently the best of the year. But the crowds dwindle, and the areas close from lack of interest, not snow. A few attempt to drown themselves, with a high success rate, in kayaks and canoes among boulders and white water. Ever the more sensible, farmers perform backbreaking labor to collect thirty-five gallons of maple sap to make one gallon of syrup to sell for $30. Few get rich doing it, but the sugaring off, or boiling process, is a social event.

Wealthy people flee until May, and the rest wait it out; drink, fritter or are fortunate enough to have regular jobs. Suicide incidents and infidelity are high. Fishing the few lakes and streams that Vermont Fish and Wildlife have not ruined by overstocking and mismanagement is not for several weeks, and golfers must wait even longer.

I am more fortunate than most. I can write stories and sometimes get paid for it. I live in interim quarters, a garage apartment with possessions crammed in from the recent sale of my house, and no kennel. The dogs live with me, bored and muddy, of course. They sleep, then pace to go out to collect more (you guessed it) mud. Skiing has lost most of its appeal after several million right turns and a corresponding number to the left. I am old and fat, so my upper legs jelly quickly, though the adage about once riding a bike does apply to skiing. Coerced by sun and friends and a free lift ticket, I had a nice morning on the mountain last week, marred only by the odd snowboard delinquent using me as a target. I even encountered my former wife skiing with the editor of a vapid gossip column for the local weekly. She will probably cover the meeting as a ground hog siting. Punxsutawney Phil appears as often in winter as I ski. Since that day it has been chilly and dark with showers and flurries, which have added several more inches to the trails. I have one more free lift ticket which I will probably give away as I soon travel three hundred miles south to train dogs, hunt turkey, play golf until the end of May. They tell me the daffodils are up. I don't have a bad life.

But for now, three restless dogs peer at me with canine petulance. I will take them for a walk.

I'm back. We drove through Moscow Village to what has proved over thirty years to be my most productive woodcock covert. On the way we pass a jogging mother pushing her infant in one of those ghastly prams made for this sort of thing. I wonder if she has consulted the baby, or if it is merely a prop for another working mother. The child's only infant memories will be of being jarred insensate over ruts in a wheeled device shepherded by a red-faced grimacing stranger. And memories of daycare, of course. We pass a temporary lake in a cornfield on which float several geese and a brace of mallards. I hope they aren't tempted to nest here, as the water will shrink to nothing. We park and walk the perimeter of the covert in a field hayed last autumn. I am struck by the comparison between this day and a day last November when I caught the last flight of woodcock. The days are similar; cool and gray, but the feel is vastly different. I annoy friends when I praise the virtues of "stick season," that wistful time between Veteran's Day and Christmas. Of course I am a hunter. Today is gaunt without promise. Limbo must look like this. Mildred, the Shorthair, home from a saturation of Texas quail, listlessly points an early return woodcock who flushes with similar lassitude. Current field trial prospect, Liver's End Arrow, runs a downwind Spaniel pattern in the open field by rote, not expecting to flush much. Tweed IV has to be helped up a bank, and I wonder what it will be like to lose my shooting pal of fourteen seasons and how I will deal with it. He is the Methuselah of Spaniel field trials, competing and placing in a gundog stake for the last four years since his open class retirement. The competition is coming up soon, and I decide not to run him if it's hot. Right before returning to the wagon Mildred joyfully rolls in a winter bounty horror so pungent as to make my eyes water on the way home. A sponge bath helps some, and now I'm ready for a nap.

I am part of a poker group that plays every Friday night, commencing with the onset of standard time and ending with daylight savings. It is not a high-stakes game, but by most standards would be considered high enough. All evening I came in second best in a series of big hands. Disheartened, I left the game, stepped on the last remaining patch of snow and fell (right again) into the mud. 'Tis a merry life and full one! I was merely damp and my sweat pants were somewhat tarnished. Mud wrestling is a recent phenomenon eclipsed by earlier contests involving fighting drunks in the parking lot of my bar in days gone by. But what of the many spills we sportsmen endure throughout our sporting lives? Careers fraught with peril and duct tape, admonished by cries of "Duck!" and "Jump Clear!"

You ride in your friend's SUV to the trailhead of a path leading to a remote pond holding native brook trout. The vehicle is equipped with one of those hellish canoe racks that sticks out eighteen inches past the side of the roof. You open your door and run directly into the same post you hit duck hunting last fall opening the same gash above your right eye. "Duck!" Still dizzy you take second position behind your partner heading down the uneven rock-strewn goat track. Slipping on a mossy boulder your partner has time to yell, "Jump Clear!" as he loses the bow. You don't. The bow bounces free and you are pitched into a scrub pine bush with needles like number 1 sandpaper and the day is still young. The shin you barked last week toppling off a wobbly step ladder you were using to locate your reel bag onto bags of poorly stored decoys comes to rest on a sharp rock. Still woozy and limping pathetically you see the end is in sight for this ghastly one-mile black-fly-infested portage. Not so fast, buckaroo. You take your eyes off the trail for only a second to savor the glittering gem of a pond, trip on a cedar root and FALL IN with the canoe on top of you. You face a day of pain in wet gear and you haven't even launched yet.

My friend, Peter, is a renowned outdoor photographer and the most spectacularly clumsy sportsman I have ever seen. Over thirty-five years I have watched him stumble, plunge and trip his way through woods and waters. He is additionally encumbered by photography bags, cameras and straps, packs loaded with accessories. A dunking for Peter is a catastrophe followed by hours of tricky reclamation and drying of his expensive gear. A capsize on the Upper Connecticut seconds after launch, a still clear picture of him standing on a stable rock windmilling his arms forward and back like Don Quixote prior to a slow motion swan dive into the Winooski River, are fond memories. Then the vision of a slogging Miller slowly pursued by the sadistic keeper of a private marsh in a pole boat. Peter's over the shoulder answer as to why he was hunting inside the posted boundaries was

"There are no ducks over there." This right before he stepped off panting into a pothole on the boundary. "That SOB herded me in there," he maintains.

I have seen two incidents of "swimming with the fishes." One intentional one not. The first was an enthusiastic young angler with his first salmon following it, rod held high, through a half-mile rapid. The other a prominent Boston attorney who slipped off a rock in Labrador and was swept around the corner to almost certain demise. His arrival alive at camp, waders filled, with grilse still miraculously attached occasioned the renaming of the home pool to "the Swimming Lawyer."

I have not gotten through my sporting life unscathed. Quite the reverse. I often state that if water didn't have fish swimming in it and ducks floating on it, I would never get near the dreadful stuff.

There is little to differentiate voluntary or involuntary fallings in. The results are the same and invariably unpleasant. Two dog rescues come to mind: Tweed II attempted, in his thirteenth year, a water retrieve of a grouse and was swept downstream with bird in mouth and into a hydraulic under a branch. The heart-stopping December water was not a consideration. In I went. Similarly the extraction of Panda from an especially virulent lake of pig manure in South Dakota. Involuntary was the swamping of a duck boat in salt skim ice on Long Island Sound when two ill trained Labrador brutes jumped into the bow and overpowered me so they could bark at a seagull. Half a mile from shore Charlie and I and, unfortunately, the Labs survived. All else was lost. One asks, "Do things like this happen often duck hunting?" The laconic answer is, "Only once." In the land of my fathers, Newfoundland, fishermen don't bother to learn how to swim, and life vests are called markers.

Fortunately God takes pity on accident-prone drunks and sportsmen, so most of us get through without major hospital time or early funeral expenses for our families. But, just to be on the safe side, that residual patch of ice I see on the first step down from the deck of my garage abode has an ominous look to it. I had best deal with it after I mix another martini.

— 9 —

Cape Breton Island • July 2001

The Next One

John Harris, if you have not fallen off the perch, which I doubt, and you happen to stumble across this book, I want you to know you are a daily inspiration to me as I play my own fifteenth hole, sixty-three years in a few days. Eight years ago you were eighty. If I still had an address I would mail a copy, but you already had more afflictions than Job in your last five years before we met, and I fear the book would be returned to sender.

I remember that your wife had died recently, that you had a coronary bypass and a colostomy within the last two years. I applauded your threat of death and dismemberment to the doctor who gave you one of those bags. They always do that, but you made him reattach everything. I don't remember too much about your life except that you were in oil, no surprise, had been a member of the Texas Border Patrol and had hunted every possible locale and critter. My remembrance is fuzzy; massive doses of tequila did this to me, but I still have the bird-carrying strap you made with your initials, JH, branded into the leather for sale in the lodge gift shop, and I remember how you shot quail. Most really big men look a little clumsy with a small 20 bore, sort of like an elephant balanced on a ball. Not you. I had come to Mexico with my friend Winney to learn to hit quail, you had shot enough that day and coached me, lending that sweet little Benelli 20 with which you seldom missed. I retained some of what you taught me. I can still see you and Winney; two three-hundred-pound Texans, you looked like bookends, riding in those spring-mounted seats on the front of the Suburban with those tiny bottles of iced Pacifico and lime in the drink holders. I also remember how much quicker you were than Winney, twenty years your junior, getting out of those seats when the dogs pointed yet another forty-bird covey.

The only time I saw you move quicker was when we would arrive back at the lodge and the staff greeted us on the veranda with frozen margaritas on a silver tray. No one ever beat you out of the truck.

I had no idea that yours was the money behind the place until the owner informed us that you had requested we stay an extra two days as your guests because you liked having us around.

I do recall wonderful meals, stories and your answer when we were sitting around late one evening and I asked you which of all your hunts was the best.

"THE NEXT ONE!"

— 10 —

SCHULTZVILLE, NEW YORK • SUMMER 1999

Barry and Quinn

If you have never treated yourself to a driven shoot in the United Kingdom make sure you do so before you get too old. Yes, the shoot is pricey unless you are an invited guest. Sometimes the company is stuffy and the traditional grouse shoot is often replaced with pheasant. One English friend maintains his own grouse moor with three year-round keepers and only enough birds to run a shoot every three years. It was because of this I met Robin, suffering avian execution withdrawal, at a shoot on Anglesey Island, Wales. He was there to shoot driven pheasant, estate raised, and to "splash a few puddlies" on the lake. Truly an A-plus gun who hosts or participates in numerous shoots each year, Robin is a marvelous source of knowledge on the traditions and form that make up a proper shoot. A lengthy discussion of attire, etiquette, guns has its place but by far the more interesting is the logistics of the shoot. There is a reason why, in a perfect drive, the birds fly steadily rather than all at once, and present "tall" and challenging targets for the guns 'til the horn is sounded ending the drive, and the beaters are within earshot of the shooters. Head keeper is an extremely prestigious title on an estate, but he is only as good as his individual beaters and their dogs. Make sure, if allowed, that you walk at least one drive with the beaters to see what goes on.

For over fifty years three of the beaters at Presaddfed Estate in Wales worked all the shoots using generations of spaniels. A testimonial by owner, Talbot Radcliff, to their dedication hangs in the hall.

Scroll of Honor
The Three Musketeers
Henri Prince – Tom Lynes – Jack Grib
50 years in the firing line. 50 years of inclement weather.
  50 years of never missing a day. 50 years of good humor
  with good springers. 50 years of giving pleasure to others.
  50 years of being jolly good fellows.
Signed – Talbot Radcliffe

Talbot died at ninety in 1999. When I asked him two years prior how eighty-eight felt he allowed as he wasn't buying any new suits. After a particularly awesome afternoon loading for Robin, the lad answered Talbot's inquiry at tea that his gun had missed but two birds all afternoon. I could not resist pointing out to Talbot that such a performance sounded like the tales of his shooting prowess in days past. Talbot replied, "I would not have missed the two." Though sometimes wrong but never in doubt, he probably would not have.

Out of the same estate from the breeding genius of this same man came the Saighton line of English Springer Spaniels, arguably the dominant breeding in U.S. field-trial success in the latter half of this century. Radcliff specialized in the American and Canadian markets, and the dogs that remain in Wales are modest, though many of the beater's dogs are of the Saighton lineage.

Breeding, training and even feeding are handled considerably more pragmatically over there. Tradition and superstition play important roles. Few trainers will ever bother with a light yellow-eyed spaniel. They cull in a fashion we would consider merciless.

Talbot said that those culled for even minor faults "grew nice roses." The plus side of this is that lines can maintain integrity for generations, whereas here we tend to make field champions of flawed dogs that pass on their faults to generations of puppies.

Barry, a member of a large Welsh family that speaks this tongue-spiraling language in the home, grew up in a cottage close to the Presaddfed Estate. He is steeped in the lore of dogs and shooting, but how could he become more than an observer? No family members were estate retained and short of the time-honored tradition of poaching, how could he be involved? The answer was a dog, which he would train himself. But even a puppy at fifty pounds would be way out of his price range.

Squatting on a corner of the estate is a charlatan who had wormed his way onto the property through Talbot's good graces. He is a trainer and was charged to keep up the Saighton line, but now he simply breeds a few dogs of his own to sell to the unsuspecting. For years eviction proceedings against him have been dragging through the courts like dead animals. Quinn was a dog of little promise and a short future. To save the cost of a cartridge, rather than give the dog to Barry, as he should have, the man sold him Quinn for five pounds—no papers.

Barry took Quinn home to the cottage. The dog was so shy he would not move from the center of the main room but stood and shook for hours. He had probably been sorely abused and starved. The steps that Barry used to win Quinn's confidence and train him to be an acceptable beater's dog can not be found in books, but only in the methods of the instinctual dog man. Nothing came easily for Quinn, but love prevailed.

My first view of the pair was at a particularly daunting sheep fence. Barry, who was small and thin for his sixteen years, was encouraging Quinn to cross. He would jump over the fence as the dog looked quizzically from the other side and listened to words of encouragement. Back and forth went the handler until finally one of the experienced beaters tired of the charade and pitched the dog over. Barry will have many better dogs, but none more devoted. Many times during the shooting activities I would see the pair in the gnarliest covert or swamp doing more than required. Barry puts in time doing other jobs with the keepers for no pay, just for the experience.

Barry has greenish blue eyes, and long blond hair, which he cut off to visit Pondview Kennels in New York. He's all boy. His favorite joke — "How do you get a cat to bark?" Answer. "Pour petrol on it and strike a match . . . Whoof." His biggest moment was when Quinn retrieved his first woodcock.

Jerry, whom I have trained with for over twenty years and is owner of Pondview Kennels, assumed a mentoring role to Barry, who visited for a summer. He worked with diligence and high humor, improved his shooting skills and dog knowledge, at all times keeping us entertained. At the end of the summer five lady clients put together a farewell party. When he left the mood was grim for a week.

I am by no means an Anglophile, but I notice a great disparity between the teenagers of our nations. Possibly rural kids of the two countries are not that different, those who grow up hunting, fishing, and working land. But the boys and girls I have met in my

U.K. travels are self-motivated and outstanding the way I hope we were in my generation. And polite. I am afraid forty years of liberal social and educational programs, the vilification of guns and hunting, culminating in the turpitude of the joint Clinton presidency might not be reversible. The bravery and love of freedom that saw us through World War II has often been replaced by cynicism and hate for this country among this confused generation of children. On the surface, despite the frenzied attempts by U.K. liberals to disarm and detraditionalize them, the young I meet on these estates and in the villages from all stations seem less infected.

There is no doubt Barry will become an estimable dog trainer; it is merely how good. With tutoring by the handler of two national champions and his own focus, excellence is a given. He is coming over again to train with us, possibly full time. The question over which he agonizes is whether to bring Quinn. I suspect boy and dog will always be together.

– 11 –

WATERBURY CENTER, VERMONT • DECEMBER 1987

Pandamonium Chronicles

Teaching an Old Campaigner a New Trail

"Give me a year and I will have the best grouse and woodcock Spaniel in New England," I bragged.

"The price was right, anyway," said my friend and professional English Springer trainer, Jerry. The match between "Panda" and me was a natural. I had lost my gun dog and sometime trial dog to a car. Panda had lost her breeder/owner in a tragic car accident returning from a field trial, and so I inherited her. It is two autumns since I made my boast, and I am a long way from my goal, but seeing daylight.

For the reader, I include here some information that may help in deciding whether or not to buy that "fully trained dog" that can be either a shortcut or a nightmare. I confess that the only breed I know well is English Springers, but I am confident much here applies to other breeds.

Panda was a whirlwind puppy who won her Open Championship in the first two trials she ran, professionally trained and handled by Jerry. Handled by her deceased owner, she was well on her way to an Amateur Championship when she ran wild.

There is no percentage in continuing to trial a dog that has a tendency to break. With a natural nose and bird sense she had been a star at a pheasant hunting club professionally handled by her old trainer. But having shared her owner's life and house, Panda was not good at kennel life; she barked continually and snapped at other dogs.

In short, I got a bargain. I had a promising pup in training for field trials and Panda filled my gundog needs, so I had the option to try for the final points on her Amateur Championship. The last achievement was doubtful, for she was soon to turn seven. She happily assumed a mother role with my male puppy, and easily slipped back into her former life of a sometime house and car dog. So far, so good.

October and as always, the woodcock arrived in Vermont and the grouse were already here. My requirements were as simple as a Russian coach who tells a highly trained acrobat, "Helga, you are older. Now you will join our rowing team."

Panda had never seen a woodcock. My previous Springers were started on woodcock at six months, long before they were steadied to flush and then hunted over at eighteen months or so. Panda only knew one speed—her trial speed—and had never hunted cover as tough as our Vermont alders. Within a week, being the trooper she was, she had hunted herself into an inguinal hernia that cost us most of the fall. Not only would I have to encourage her to adopt a different pace, within a reasonable time frame I had to install new bird sense. Her retrieving and marking were fine, but trial range was not alder swamp range. She quartered machinelike, barely in gun range, and flushed the poor timberdoodles with the speed and aggression that helped her win trials. Her range I could control with work but the flush I could not, nor did I want to. If I could stop her from "punching out" I would have to learn to read her better and tune my waning fifty-year-old reflexes to her flush. The two of us in our second season have made progress and have reached a point where with some fine adjustments we will be a good team. To break the pattern, I had to experiment and insult the old champ by putting her back on a check cord with my foot on it frequently to limit her distance—basic but effective. Making sure of her conditioning to avoid further damage, I would send her into the heaviest cover I could find early in the hunt. This had the predictable effect of slowing her trial speed. Quite by accident I found that she had never been belled, and the fastening of the same shortened her range to almost painfully close. This was a lucky stroke, and the bell could be used as a reminder when she punched out. At the same time I refused to let her get sloppy and break at the flush or before she was sent to retrieve. When she tried this she received not gentle correction reminiscent of her early training. The most important breakthrough came naturally. We started to take birds and for the first time in her life she understood hunting for the gun.

Two types of finished dogs are spun off and might be available secondhand to the hunter. First is the reject—the dog that, for some reason, flunks out of school because it does not show potential as a top gun or trial dog. This could be good or bad. Find out the reason why the dog is for sale! If it is that it simply lacks the drive to make it to the top, the dog may make an excellent gun dog. If the dog has problems that developed during training, or a severe fault it brought to the party on its own; be careful as these dogs are hard to correct. The worst aberration is gun shyness. Others could include: failure to retrieve, undue stubbornness, poor nose, hard mouth, physical defects, and on and on. Ask the dog's history, get a vet's health certificate and if possible get the seller to allow you to see the dog work in a controlled training situation.

The second type is the "grand old campaigner," portrayed by Panda. These dogs are available less often, because they are kept for breeding purposes or as old friends and gun dogs by the original owners.

With both types, know as much as possible about the dog and your own training abilities to enable you to make a sound choice. The obvious alternative is to buy a pup or started dog and work with a professional trainer. This is particularly advisable if the dog is to be your first venture. Do not forget that the trained dog will come with his own already formed traits, and remember that a trial dog is accustomed to experienced handling.

Panda and I just returned from a South Dakota pheasant hunt where we served as guides. She loved working those big familiar roosters again and did it to perfection. More than one of our clients offered to buy her for far more than fair market value, but I declined. Even though she hasn't placed in a single trial so far this year, who can say she won't? And think of the problems I am saving a new owner by keeping her for myself.

FC Panda Bear of Awarrinigton 1980–1995
(FROM *Spaniels in the Field*, FALL 1995.)

Summer heat and extreme old age terminated a genetic experiment and the life of one of the strangest Spaniels ever to flush a rooster.

I was her third owner. Her breeder, Nick Yozzo, had attempted to accomplish a modern miracle: a dual champion, show and field. One entire side was a venerable show line. Though there are duals in the distant past, specialized breeding programs render this goal increasingly improbable.

At the time of Nick's death Panda was four years old, an open field champion with three wins including the Parent Club. She certainly had a show look, though I suspect spectators would have thrown pie at her in the ring.

She was briefly owned by the legendary Evelyn Monte. Nobody wanted her so she came cheap to fill my gun dog needs. Her conversion to woodcock and grouse was the subject of the article reprinted on pages 58–61. I trialed her occasionally, though she never had another placement, except in water trials at which she excelled, winning one in her eleventh year. From her stubby two-inch tail to her lopsided running style she was an anachronism. Trial dogs became flashier and faster, frequently outrunning their nose, something Panda never did.

Where Panda stood apart was in her colossal weirdness. Her brain circuits could have supplied special effects in a Stephen King movie. Ray Cacchio only admits to being her trainer under oath. She detested him in return. Ray's greatest fear is that the oil painting of Panda, which I have willed to him, might arrive before he can leave the county without a forwarding address. She was a solemn dog with no interest in play, toys, other dogs or people other than me. She ate every meal as if it were her last, and would stare at the refrigerator by the hour. She despised puppies, though she raised one litter very competently, I am told. None of them amounted to much, so my first act of ownership was to have her spayed. Though not aggressive toward humans or other dogs she guarded my car and home, leaving no doubt as to her intentions should an intruder test her resolve. She never started a dog fight, but finished them quickly by fastening on to the adversary's nose.

Gardening was her passion. The only garden vegetable she would not eat raw was celery. Once under the fence she could devour entire rows of asparagus, her favorite.

Panda was a big dog, with a trial weight of forty-two pounds; sometimes she ballooned to almost sixty, with paws and hips as big as all outdoors. Her Brillo-like fur resembled a yak in winter. She was victim of continuous allergies and undiagnosable medical problems that she bore with stoic resignation.

Panda was the clumsiest animal I have ever seen. She constantly tripped, fell and ran into things. Her greatest triumph was in South Dakota, where she toppled into a cesspool of pig waste from which I had to rescue her by wading in up to my armpits.

Suffice it to say she was a bird dog with incredible endurance and tenacity. One of her best years was her thirteenth season— totally deaf, half blind and stiff in the joints.

She helped guide paid hunts in Iowa, South Dakota, Nebraska, Kansas and New York. Clients offered sums for her I would have been embarrassed to accept. Though a flawless retriever of ducks and geese, one hour of her moaning in the blind was all I could stand. At age eleven she completed forty-six retrieves on pheasants in one afternoon at a tower release in Quebec. She was the finest tracker of running and wounded birds I have ever seen.

And on and on . . . it is unlikely that Nick's noble breeding experiment will be repeated, and sad in a way that a dual champion is now such an unreality. But if you know of some girl with a heart as big as her butt and a side of show, let me know. If nobody wants her I'd be interested.

— 12 —

WATERBURY CENTER, VERMONT • NOVEMBER 1998

Feist Dog Squirrels

I remember visiting in the Adirondacks as a twelve-year-old and shooting red squirrels for bounty. They were such an annoyance and so destructive camp owners would pay us fifty cents for each tail. I never thought of eating a squirrel until an ill-fated duck-hunting trip, when a planned duck dinner did not materialize. We shot a fat gray squirrel and fried it. Though it was tasty it took me thirty years to shoot another one over one thousand miles south of Vermont in Mississippi.

The plantation lies partially in Mississippi and partially in Alabama. Mr. Robert is the steward of these lands and farms it as generations of his family have. They take their responsibilities to the land, those who work it, and the fish and game thereon seriously. Overshoot a covey of quail and you will not be invited again. The quantity of game is staggering. The state allows a hunter thirty deer in a season, but not Robert. A cadre of friends, among them the Judge, has been hunting here since they were young boys. Dove shoots for up to three hundred have been held there with tents, Southern barbecue and drink. Children barely as tall as the guns they shoot knock down doves with frightening ease. It is a good thing for the North it had the industrial might in the War Between the States, if all was decided by marksmanship we would have separate nations today.

As with any activity indulged excessively, now that these men are in their fifties enthusiasm wanes. Speaking of deer hunting and turkeys, which he calls by mouth, the Judge puts it simply, "I'm not as mad at 'em as I used to be." But get him on hunting squirrels with his Feist Dog and he imparts all the enthusiasm of his youth. These men who have shot everything available are nuts on squirrels. They cherish the opportunity to go to camp with their kids and share this smallest of game with them using small-bore rifles and shotguns.

Feist Dogs are a passion of the Deep South, where they are carefully bred and seriously competed. They are fierce, mid-sized, terrier-type dogs, sturdy with deep chests and brindle colored. Exactly what the genetics are, who knows. They will never be a recognized breed by AKC. Years ago I answered the door at my in-laws' West Virginia home. On the porch was a diminutive wrinkled black man with a tiny Beagle pup in his arms. He informed me that he had heard that the Doctor's rabbit dog had died. The Doctor had done much pro bono orthopaedic work on this man's family, paid for in vegetables and such and now with this puppy. I commented on the quality of the dog, ascertained that he bred dogs for the entire county and asked if they were all purebred. "Some are and the rest are pretty well Beaglified." For want of better description these Fiest dogs are pretty well Terrierfied.

On my way up from Texas in late February, the only season still open was gray squirrel. We were to meet "Tiny," who had started as offensive tackle for Mississippi State and can be distinguished from his Daddy, "Big Tiny," who is five-feet-six and weighs 140 pounds. At the entrance to the camp road the NO NUTTIN' sign, which reads NO HUNTIN', NO FISHIN', NO TRESPASSIN', NO NUTTIN'. It means every word.

Along the Tom Bigbee River on high ground in a Cyprus Swamp is the spacious camp with bunks for ten and every convenience. Back out the camp road is the vast squirrel and turkey woods, mostly oaks providing unlimited acorns. In camp prodigious amounts of fried redfish and what my Southern friends call Yankee whiskey—martinis. We stay up late as there is no reason to get up early, a civilized hunt starts a ten A.M. The three of us sally forth into spring sunshine with Scrappy, the Feist dog. The Judge is an estimable dog trainer of any kind of dog.

Hugh, a Welsh Trainer of champion Sheepdogs once told me, "Even a poor trainer might have a good dog in his lifetime. A good trainer will always have one or more fine dogs in his kennel."

Those who know about these specialized canines say Scrappy is the best they have ever seen. I don't know whether the Judge bothers to trial him or not. Around camp he is quiet and well behaved but on the command "Find 'em" he takes off like a rocket was up his rear. We sit down on a log and wait. Within minutes he starts a constant bark that he will continue until we saunter up. The rifleman with a rapid-fire .22 auto will try to pick the gray off but usually the prey will start scampering around and through the trees, jumping twenty feet or more, making a sporting shot for the man with the .410. When the squirrel drops to the ground Scrappy runs over to investigate and if alive gives it a quick death shake after which he would show no further interest.

We would often find the dog looking up and by following his line of sight, which is extremely keen, determine the quarry was in a hole. At this point the rifleman would rapid fire at the hole, sometimes flushing out the rodent. If not the Judge would give the command "Gone in a hole" and Scrappy would be off for the next inhabited tree.

The entire performance provided challenge, laughs and a pile of squirrels. There is no easy way to skin a squirrel. The skin clings to the meat with a death grip relieved only by sippin' whiskey for the skinner. But oh, are they worth it. Most good squirrel recipes call for long and slow cooking, which allows for more whiskey and an extended afternoon nap. Here are two of the Judge's best recipes.

Squirrel in Low Gravy

I asked the Judge if "low" referred to the Low Country of the Deep South. He maintains it refers to the reduction by the slow simmering process.

Cut squirrels into four quarters at each leg. A fifth piece is made by cutting both sides of the backbone. Dredge in flour. Season with garlic powder, salt and pepper. Brown in peanut oil in an iron skillet. Set aside the browned pieces. Out of the drippings and flour construct a mocha-colored roux thinned with strong bouillon. Reserve the broth to add as needed. Place meat and roux in ovenware vessel. Two chopped onions, Worcestershire sauce, chopped garlic, a stick of butter, baby carrots. In the oven at 200 for three hours, adding reserved liquid as needed. Meat will be falling off the bone into a thick dark gravy. Serve with rice and biscuits.

Brunswick Stew

Any combination of chicken, pork and squirrel boiled to bone. Cube and brown in peanut oil. Add the following either fresh, frozen or canned: stewed tomatoes, lima or butter beans, celery, corn, onion, garlic, cayenne pepper, salt and pepper. Simmer on stovetop, adding water as needed. I like to cook dumplings on top during last stage.

    The woods around my house in Hollowville are full of grays. Though delicious, the labor-intensive skinning protects them from this lone and lazy sportsman.

— 13 —

New York City • May, 1983

Should We Take the Clay Shooters Hunting?

There is great hoopla about sporting clays these days. If my facts are sketchy so be it. An opinion column is by definition subjective, and I intend to take full advantage of that latitude.

Sporting clays first became popular in Britain. Not an offshoot of skeet or trap, it is a game simulating situations that could be encountered in a day's shooting. The stations are named: springing teal, bounding rabbit, gliding bluebills, but the targets are still clay. I can say, from my limited experience, that the targets are very difficult. Though never a threat, at one time I maintained a nineties average in registered skeet. The two times I have attempted this new discipline my scores were in the humbling thirties. There is no question that I could become addicted; many of my friends are. I have neither the funds nor the time to support such an addiction, so I respectfully decline. If it doesn't have feathers I will abstain, except for the odd outing where my goal will be to break over thirty targets.

There is little doubt that sporting clays is going to be big in this country, but just how big remains to be seen. Philosophically there is nothing in the pursuit of clays that has anything to do with hunting and gathering. Sporting clays seems to be closer to golf, with its handicaps and scoring. Spanish philosopher Ortega Y. Gasset, whose treatise on hunting specifies that game must be shot, would write off sporting clays as mere extraneous target practice. Current aficionados mostly spring from the ranks of hunters, but this will not always be the case. I predict a future group of shooters who have never hunted, some of whom will wish to move from clay to the real thing. What will be the hunter's obligation to them? The sport will spawn a group of shooters with marvelously honed skills and not a clue about the pursuit of game.

Safety. The stations are generally little boxes that confine the shooter, making it all but impossible to swing and spray. Would you feel comfortable with one of these guys in a woodcock cover with your best dog?

Ethics. Though I have yet to shoot in the United Kingdom, I feel that the Brits are prone to regard game as targets to be privately estate-harvested without limits. This does not mean they don't respect the quarry, but it is far different from a sporting clay shooter. What ethics will this shooter bring to the live game party? I have already had a taste of this. One of my duties working for a major outdoor magazine was to coordinate the shooting and fishing outings for our advertising clients. Tough duty, eh? Jim Carmichel, the well-known gun editor, and I ran an annual dove shoot in Tennessee attended by some very heavy hitters and people from their ad agencies. At the most recent event, one of the invited was a personable young man from an agency in the Midwest who readily admitted no experience with game but a fair amount with clays. He went off by himself, and throughout the afternoon I heard an inordinate amount of shooting from his position. During a lull in the action I decided to investigate. He was surrounded by more than half a case of hulls and few dove. When I questioned him it turned out that he had been shooting at anything that came by—meadowlarks, robins, blackbirds. The field was littered with their carcasses and he saw nothing wrong. I was livid, but controlled my anger, and informed him that this was not acceptable, and that some of the birds he was shooting were protected by heavy fines. He thanked me, and proceeded to shoot at dove only, quickly filling his limit. In short, he did not know he was violating any rules or ethics. Are we to be deluged in the field by shooters like this young man? I shudder, and so did Emerson Hough, who wrote the following in 1915; it appeared in the publication *Out of Doors.*

> The development of the sport of trap-shooting at targets has kept us Americans in the front rank of users of the shotgun in spite of the gradual disappearance of our opportunities for field-shooting. In the old days of general abundance of wild game, the average man in this country could learn to shoot in the field. In the Old World, skill with the shotgun has long been an accomplishment belonging to relatively few, and those of the privileged classes. Today our lessening game supply has deprived us of much of the popular enjoyment of field sports once so general, so that although today more Americans own shotguns than ever before, and although they are better trap-shots than the world ever before saw, still we have lost standing as a race of good wing shots, odd as that paradox may sound.
>
> Trapshooting at targets seems rather mechanical to the man following his own gun and dog. It perfects the skill of any user of the shotgun, and it has become so general in America that our better amateur trap-shots best those of any

nation. In Europe the sport of trap-shooting is not made a business, as it is here. Targets thrown from towers, from behind hedges and screens, at unexpected angles, are there thought to afford better practice for the shotgun than the systematic target grinding of the average American tournament.

The antis are not going to go away. Their nose is in the tent. In Britain, where shooting, and particularly fox hunting, is high profile elitist, without a National Rifle Association to fight for them, the entire camel has taken up residence. I recently saw a quote from a Dame Snoot Face or some such handle, whose arrogant pronouncement was, "If they must shoot, let them shoot sporting clays." If the antis can confine us to sporting clays clubs and to game farms they can control us. Containment, ammunition price gouging, banning certain types of firearms, then outlawing all firearms is the ethical sportsman's death knell.

Should we take the clay specialists hunting? Maybe, but make them pay their dues. They will come to us with nothing but their guns, ammo, and boots. All else we will have to supply; trained dogs, guiding and the many things it has taken a lifetime to acquire. There should be no shortcuts. I have taken on the awesome responsibility of educating a couple of my godsons and I take this very seriously. I may overdo it, but by the time they are carrying a loaded gun they have walked endless miles with an unloaded gun. They have been schooled, sometimes harshly, in safety, ethics and tradition. Only when I am convinced I would welcome a day in the field as their shooting companion do they load their gun.

Take the clay shooters hunting, but make them earn their stripes.

Addendum
December 12, 2000

I had forgotten I had written this pedantic tome. I came across it in a bunch of old stories and magazines I saved for one reason or another. In 1983 I was working for *Outdoor Life*. *Shotgunner's* was one of the many "gun books" that came and went in the 1980s. I assume I met the editor at an industry cocktail party and in a moment of weakness agreed to do this guest article.

    Ah! If only I were able to predict the stock market with such accuracy. The United Kingdom has, for all intents and purposes, been disarmed. In this country sportsmen and the arms industry have barely survived eight years of the Clintons' assault on their constitutional rights. And as to innovation: I recently was a spectator at a sporting clays competition at which the contestants used golf carts to transport them between stations. Give me my dog, a pocketful of shells, my 20, and a woodcock cover thick with alders, barren of rules, regulations, sporting types, and . . . golf carts.

— 14 —

Hondo, Texas • January 2000

Horror Moving

As I write this the horror, which forced me to flee my frozen Vermont home to South Texas where it is frequently over 80 degrees in January, is still fresh. Here I seek solace in abundant dove, quail and ducks and to rejuvenate my shot nerves with golf and dog training.

You see, last autumn I placed my home of twelve years on the market thinking it would take at least a year to sell. It sold in four days and I faced the prospect of MOVING. The quick sale should not have surprised me. The log house sat on a gorgeous chunk of rural Vermont with a trout brook; bird coverts were laced throughout. The purchasers, a retired couple from urban New Jersey, neither hunt nor fish and I wish them well.

Only a sportsman can relate to the trauma of an imminent move. The Latin for baggage is *impedimenta*—a colostomy bag of junk, gear and treasures pertaining to our activities. Boxes of junk that have a life of their own follow us through the years like hungry blackflies.

Compounding the seriousness of my plight was my lineage of

inveterate collectors. Childhood memories are of chaotic moves to rented homes with my parents. My grandmother and her unmarried son hauled about several warehouses full of furnishings, some of it wonderful antiques from my grandmother's Southern home that was staffed by former slaves. When my parents finally built a nest of their own they vowed never to leave it. Decades later, when my mother died, the tiny house had become a hiding place for possessions that, as with many old people, had taken over their lives. Fear and denial of the awesome mess created an Augean Stable, which culminated in a massive free garage sale and also filled a 20-yard trash container. Standouts in the mélange were cartons of ruined children's books, some valuable, and a cache of unopened wedding presents from the 1930s. The task complete and a young bond trader and family in residence, I left embittered, vowing never to so much as drive past what had been home since the age of eight. I returned to my own cluttered world in Vermont.

My first act after signing the sales agreement to my Vermont home was to run away to my fishing camp in Nova Scotia, positive the deal would fall through. It didn't. I had the foresight to set the closing for the end of November, allowing me a chance to savor a last bird hunting season in that most glorious month. Of course, I did nothing but order a dumpster into which I chucked only the worst of the gear: ski poles without baskets, cracked decoy heads, a bag of cheap spinning tackle welded together by rust. I would awake with a start at night, return to the dumpster and retrieve a discarded dog collar from a long dead Spaniel. I took to wandering about like Macbeth, muttering from room to room, glass in hand.

And the papers: a sea of correspondence, writing published and not, unpaid bills from the sixties; I have no living relatives except possibly in Newfoundland, so the smallest clipping or snapshot is that of a ghost demanding attention. One jumbled file box of my mother's I opened briefly after her funeral. A file tab jumped out at me, "Teddy's Divorce." What other debilitating tidbits could such a horror file contain? I slammed the top shut like a door on a Jehovah's Witness's foot. I'll never have the courage to read anything in that file box. But throw it away? Never.

Entire steel cases packed with hunting, fishing and skiing info. Places visited and those that never will be. Herter's catalogs from 1970. Twenty copies of the fourth and last issue of a magazine, *Rod and Gun*, that I sold advertising for, and which targeted a phantom market of wealthy sportsmen newsstand buyers. I was able to relegate a bunch of this to the landfill, but not all.

The worst millstones of all: the 700 remaining pairs of nylon knickers (Breeks) dyed a bilious oak hue, which I purchased as a closeout, six years prior, convinced the knicker would regain its former glory with shooters, golfers, and cross-country skiers. Oh yes, then there was the six-thousand pound 1954 Bentley with frozen brakes.

I hired a crew of friends, who were instructed to ignore my bleatings for mercy and forge ahead. I consumed oceans of gin and contributed little. In the middle of this dark hour a litter of puppies was born on the living-room floor; my split-second timing to transport the mother to a different birthing site was off by twenty-four hours. The moving van arrived with the first heavy snow, got stuck repeatedly, but managed to haul the big stuff to an interim apartment.

Returning home to a coward's welcome from a driven shoot in Scotland over Thanksgiving, I viewed the last boxes of incidentals packed by others. Taking up a marker I peered in one of the boxes. It contained a miasma of loose shot shells, some field trial ribbons, and several suits from a past life as a writer for outdoor magazines in New York. Realizing I would be unable to fit my leg in the waistband today, I dug deeper. A Tynor original of a brace of woodcock dropping through perfect sticks to a stream, one hunting sock and a cracked dog bowl. I decided to mark the container "Miscellaneous." Six almost identical cartons later, each emblazoned with a scarlet "M," I was raving like King George. One of those silly adages that makes much sense is: after a move if you have any unopened boxes six months later throw them out, as they obviously are extraneous. Fat Chance! I needed all of this, I howled. Mildred the Shorthair, who moments before had been lying forlornly in the middle of what had been her den, covered her ears with her paws.

"Come on, Girl. Let's get this stuff in the truck. Six days from now we'll be in Texas where we belong."

— 15 —

CAPE BRETON ISLAND • JUNE 2002

Fishing Buddies

I don't really have one, which is my loss. There are several friends I fish with, and a couple have attained "buddy" status for brief periods under five years, so the relationship does not really wash. A true fishing buddy is not a casual friend or necessarily a social one. You may only see him in fishing situations once or twice a year, but the bond is often stronger than your marriage. Years ago a seasoned combat veteran defined a real friend as one you would want to be in a firefight with. Fishing is not much different. There are life-threatening incidents with boats, motors, vehicles and miscellaneous gear perversely attempting to wreck your trip. I have a fishing friend who years ago approached nervous collapse when the cooling line for the transmission in my wagon broke, spraying the block, which filled the cab with black smoke. This was easily repaired, but his reaction confirmed "friend" not "buddy" for the duration. After all, the car had little brake and a power-steering unit that had been dry for months. What's a little pungent smoke while returning from a salmon escapade?

A buddy is stoic through flat tires, rain and bugs, busted travel plans and lousy fishing. He contributes equally to the kitty, does his share in camp and anticipates your moods and the small things that need to be done without being asked. If the two of you take trips together, the teamwork has to withstand delayed flights, incompetent guides, lost gear ("I have an extra set") and incompatible jerks that are attached to your party. The fishing buddy bond must survive the slings and arrows of outrageous fortune time and time again.

Dwight and Sam were veterans of many camps and trips. Both were successful in their Maine businesses; Dwight was a researcher and Sam owned an insurance agency. Dwight collected and traded stamps; Sam restored antique cars. They had little in common except for forty years of trout fishing together. When Dwight died Sam took his ashes and sprinkled them on a Maine pond from the deck of the camp they shared for so many years. I understand Sam still does a bit of fishing, but not a lot.

Dan and Ed met in their forties. Ed was a recovering alcoholic looking for an outlet. They both worked for Maine banks and played world-class cribbage. Dan took on Ed and taught him from scratch the arcane art of Maine pond fishing for brookies. On a trip Dan consumes Bourbon Manhattans, "with an orange but no cherry" and Ed drinks a tree bark-flavored Maine soft drink called Moxie. The ribbing is constant, the competition fierce. Ed now fishes with equal skill; he even suggests they are no longer equal.

I am happy to have introduced Matt and Tony twenty years ago. They are wealthy and of retirement age and they share a passion for adventure fishing of which most can only dream. Both have houses and boats in Florida. Between them they belong to, or have access to, the most exclusive fishing clubs in the world and understanding wives who allow such indulgence. Patagonia,

Costa Rica, Labrador. They will be in camp here on the way back from a remote Salmon River in Labrador which few have ever fished. The trip could go either way, but they risk it comfortable in each other's company, and the fact that they have survived the worst over the years. "Bring it on!"

Bruce and Butch share the financial independence that allows fishing fantasy trips but little else. Butch made his fortune in the flamboyant ski industry. Bruce in plumbing fixtures for the handicapped. They were in college together over forty years ago and started fishing then. Butch entertained Bruce in his vintage Rangeley Lake camp in the days when Maine trout were a viable resource on the big popular lakes. They had businesses to run and families to raise. Now in the enviable position of having sons do the day-to-day at their successful businesses, they go to Russia, South America, and the Arctic whenever they wish. They are truly fishing's odd couple. Unless you know them well the ribbing that Butch bestows upon his more laconic buddy is almost uncomfortable to be around. It is a relationship that has worked for decades; neither would have it any other way.

I am too old now to acquire a buddy. After all, these liaisons require a test of time, not a viable option at my age. But I can console myself by partaking in a few of the trips these fishing buddies share.

— 16 —

HOLLOWVILLE, NEW YORK • MARCH 2002

English Barney

The kennel with which I am associated, Pondview, brings dogs—Cockers, Labs and Springers—in from the United Kingdom. Our contact now is Ian, the owner of a world-renowned kennel and line of field champions. Before this we brought over the Saighton line until the founder, Talbot Radcliff, died in 1999 at age ninety. As did Talbot, Ian has a sharp eye for the U.S. market and the type of dog we eagerly snap up. He comes over with up to eight dogs and leaves with a pocket full of cash. The Spaniels are all over the lot: finished trial dogs, started pups, gun dogs and dogs that are not suited for English competition because of what we see as minor faults. Trainers in the United Kingdom must present perfect dogs. A small squeak of excitement when at heel is cause for dismissal from a trial. Big, running-style American dogs are not proper there, but can be very desirable here, coming from impeccable English breeding. Recently Dan, the head trainer, brought Barney over to Pondview. Barney fits into the "spec dog" category; we don't know how he will turn out. His fault is size. Big Spaniels are not sought after over there, and he is a big friendly boy. He, however, runs with plenty of "Spaniel action"—not flat like a setter. I had my eye on him when cleaning runs and when we had him up in the training field. His size, big head and athleticism remind me of Tweed IV, whom I lost last year. His temperament, fortunately, is not the same; I no longer have the strength of will to trial a blockheaded clown like Tweed. Barney is two years old with an impressive pedigree. He has had some training; it is difficult to tell how far along he is. He is very keen. He refuses reward treats in the field while working; he is too busy doing his job as he now sees it.

Some dogs are natural kennel dogs and are perfect living their entire lives in a run, adequately provided with food, shelter and an opportunity to work. Others, and we suspect Barney is one, respond brilliantly to a home environment and "one on one." Dan agrees that he is one of these. I need a dog work in progress, so Barney came home with me last night.

Kennel dogs who have never seen a toy or the inside of a house are generally in a state of arrested social development. Some can never be acclimated to the home. They break things, spray the furniture to define territory and end up back in the kennel to which they are suited. Barney's debut was not a good one. He immediately grabbed Arrow's ball, and she snapped, frightening him so he piddled on the carpet.

We are in a perfect house for this kind of experiment. Arrow, who won a ribbon in a national championship last year, has been retired to hunt and raise a litter. We are so bonded that, like many old couples, we communicate by a form of telepathy. She sleeps on the bed and her girth is increasing. We are by ourselves since I have lost or sold the others in the last year. Though often kenneled during the day, my dogs—up to six—live in the house with me when I am home. The house is small, so they have to be calm and get along to avoid canine bedlam.

This year we moved from Vermont down to mid New York State to get out of the snow and to be closer to Pondview and the East Coast hub of Spaniel activity. My new home consists of two camps on four acres with a training field and small stream. The kennel will be built this summer. The more elegant of the two camps is not winterized, so we are in the rustic one. Carpeted with ancient indoor-outdoor carpet and cast-off furniture from Pondview, I sleep in a sleeping bag on a couch. There is little Barney can do while learning house manners to disturb the décor. After a while last night he lay calmly across the tiny main room and watched me. A very good sign. He slept quietly in a crate in the other room. At six A.M. we hunted the property perimeter down to the creek. He frequently checked in to me for approval, another good sign. As I type he lies under the table next to my foot with what is now his ball. Kennel aromatherapy wafts upward, promising a bath at Pondview tomorrow.

I have a good feeling about this big Englishman and his future. His first step will be socialization and lots of walks, which will take on the aspects of a hunt. He will be encouraged in his back and forth out front pattern and use of wind. We will perfect heel and sit. Stay will be enforced leading to sit/stay on thrown dummies, pigeons and pheasants. We'll play games. I'll hide stuff to which he will learn to take a line and retrieve. He'll hunt dead and direct to the fall. When I am satisfied we will return to the training field at Pondview for shot birds and advanced training. He may make a trial dog, though only one of twenty-five trained for competition is ever successful. Or he will live with a loving family providing sport and game for them for the next ten years or more. What is wrong with that?

Addendum
April, 2004

Barney completed his training and entered two field trials with unspectacular results. I kept him, though I was offered large sums more than once. He earns his keep guiding with me and sleeps in the house.

– 17 –

Hollowville, New York • November 2002

Field Trials and Tribulations

I am in a quandary as to writing this chapter; I am too close to the subject and the many friends who are involved in trialing Spaniels, and not all I have to say is complimentary. Competing with dogs is a microcosm of much that is wrong with us: the politics, correctness, regimentation, bureaucratic control, polarization, bickering and violent confrontation verbal and at times physical. Though my knowledge does not extend past Spaniel trials I assume the Labs and Pointers share many of the problems exacerbated by cash prizes, which is not a part of the Spaniel game.

American Spaniel trialing began in the 1920s on Fisher's Island, New York. Exclusive is understatement for this place; duPonts, Firestones, Prestons *et al.* have summer places there. The golf course is rated the most private in America. Henry Ferguson was patron saint, holding the first Spaniel trials on this enclave. Clubs evolved on the mainland in New York and Connecticut with many of the same players involved and others of the upper crust joining them. These were the days when every sporting event was an excuse for a tailgate party. Most of the dogs were trained and handled by professional trainers, many from the United Kingdom. The owners imbibed martinis, nibbled watercress sandwiches (without crusts) and deviled eggs and watched the event from a safe distance. Though there were exceptions, by today's standards the dogs were not particularly good. If they found their birds, did not chase them into the next county and refrained from biting the judge, the dog had a good chance for one of four placements. The field was small, less than twenty dogs the norm. The awards parties were lavish and wet. Inevitably, more owners became interested in running their dogs so an amateur class was added; they could compete among themselves with largely professionally trained Spaniels but not against the professionals. A few of the owners actually did some training. One of them is quoted, "A man should not be allowed to sire children until he successfully trains a Spaniel."

There was not a middle-class. Jerry, whose last name ends in a vowel, was not invited to the awards party. One of the committee gave him his ribbon in the parking lot. He was a kid, and this was the first Springer that he had trained himself. Almost forty years later he has won two Nationals, judged over forty trials, made twenty or so field champions; some for those who were inside at that long-ago banquet. Some have begged him to campaign their dogs to no avail. He picks his dogs and his clients. But if you live long enough you get to see altered or destroyed the things about which you are most passionate. Jerry, though still judging and training the odd dog, has moved on to consulting. "The competition just isn't fun any more."

And what fun it was! With a cast of colorful characters, professional and amateur, who defined our sport. One legendary pro could turn any event into a rodeo. Having left the awards cocktail party and driven two hours to his home he staggered in to a ringing phone. He had let his eight dogs out for a run prior to the drive.

"Luke, we have your dogs here."

"I thought it was awful quiet back there."

Judges would arrive at the trial site, Hagenesque, with their dates from the previous evening still wearing their high heels.

A scion of the original Fisher's Island crowd had her staff prepare elegant treats for after-trial festivities that on this occasion was in a Holiday Inn suite. Most had departed and a plate of smoked wild duck canapés lingered on one of the beds. The hostess, a death grip on her water glass of vodka, staggered backward and planted her bony behind onto the plate. Her husband, Jim, missed not a beat, "Look Darling, pressed duck."

And Billy, with several of her stylish lady friends running dogs in riding habit. Noel breeds Cockers today from the famous line her mother founded.

The numbers of national stake placements in the open by amateurs against the pros bears testimony to big changes. Many of these handlers train their own dogs. Some hire an ethical pro, wait until they have a promising puppy fully trained, take it over to run and say they trained it. The eighties were pivotal for the dogs and their owners. Pickups replaced station wagons, breeks by blaze orange and blue jeans with prominent half moons peeking below the T-shirts.

I am one of a small cadre of retros who when they judge or compete still wear a tie. Some of us wear breeks, which are still de rigueur at trials in Britain. I think we are generally regarded at best as eccentrics; those who follow our lead are, at worst, elitists and Anglophiles. And the trial Springer Spaniel has evolved into something very different from a gentleman's close-ranging shooting dog. There are judges who prefer speed and athleticism to bird finding and control. Lord help the genetics. Fortunately, in the new millennium this trend is waning but for how long? We have created an athletic elite where average kids who enjoy sports need not apply. "No sports for you, seven-year-old, get back to your computer!" Pity the poor sod running a proper dog.

Addendum
Pondview, Schultzville, New York • March, 2003

Dan just returned from a judging assignment in the Midwest. He was compelled to preface his awards by a speech greeted by stunned silence. He questioned what had happened to the game. Impeccably dressed, he pointed out that dogs were barking under judgment, crushing birds, unable to sit still prior to being sent to quest.

There is no doubt that the top dogs are finer performers than ever before. Regional trials have close to eighty entries with half of the dogs not trained to field trial placement standards. The National Championships, in which compete the best of the best, showcase the top dogs and what may be right for the breed.

Dan says, "Most of the old guard are dead, but I am young and passionate enough to make a difference."

— 18 —

KATONAH, NEW YORK • JANUARY 1978

The Last Grouse on Pea Pond Road

Above the two-hundred-year-old spring house at my parent's home my aged Spaniel, Tweed II, flushed the most perfect specimen of cock grousedom ever beheld. The tail is framed with appropriate accolades in my Vermont home. I should never have shot him. What would have been his preferred escape route was blocked by a new twelve-foot wire fence surrounding the horse complex of a new residence on the west corner of our five acres. In the past decade what was once game lands have been slowly developed within the parameters of four-acre zoning to the point where it is not suitable to shoot here. The year before the subject grouse's demise I shot a woodcock on our property. Mrs. Humphrey's nurse came puffing down the road, frantically waving her arms and shouting that I had taken out my neighbor's bay window. I allowed this was impossible, as I knew where the house was and would never shoot in that direction. Also, I had been well over safe range from the dwelling when I shot. An inspection of the crime scene with attendant police revealed a very dead grouse below the shattered window. It had flushed and flown uphill when

I shot the woodcock. I insisted on paying for glass replacement, which Mrs. Humphrey refused. The widow of a shooter and a great sport she asked only that I dress and pluck it so she could enjoy it for her supper. Other new residents are not as understanding and holler into the woods, call the local cops and post land with angry neon signs on every tree. This last grouse was a bird of almost three pounds whose legs were dental proof. The creeping sprawl would have provided a slower and sadder end than did my .20 gauge. The location known as the Township of Bedford, New York, is where I grew up, only a commuter-train ride to New York City. It is protected by four-acre zoning and very private rich folk. Bedford was a spectacular place to be a boy in the fifties. The weather patterns were different then. There was skiing on Merrill's or Righter's Hills with reliable snow from Christmas until March, and ice-skating and hockey on White's Pond, where I learned the sport from the three great Baldwin Brothers, who had played at St. Paul's School and Harvard. We played golf and tennis at a venerable country club not far from the spreading boughs of the Bedford Oak, where they used to hang horse thieves. All heady stuff for a twelve year old. The area was laced with streams and dotted with ponds, not to mention a vast reservoir system for Manhattan, all full of fish.

At age eight I found myself living in a tiny rented house abutting acres of undeveloped swamp where I trapped muskrats. My family was reeling from the recent loss of my eleven-year-old brother and the patriarch, my Newfoundlander grandfather. It was a fine spot to enjoy solitude with BB gun and an imaginary friend who stayed with me almost to my teens. Also provided was my first chaperoned movie date with my next-door neighbor, Alice (Ali was her stage name) McGraw. We were constant playmates with her younger brother Richard. Our mothers, Ali's is an

Iroquois, took us to the beach in Connecticut when polio scares were not in the news. In no way able to appreciate Ali as anything other than a buddy at the time, I now realize too late that she was and is to this day one of the beautiful women of the century. As a child she was ethereal as well as very smart. Her father, a commercial artist with talent unrewarded by the Madison Avenue firms for which he worked, did a gratis drawing of my brother from a snapshot, which captured the occult side of this boy the camera never showed.

The shooting sport personae of this community were legion. There were Whitneys, Prestons, Randebrocks, Lambs, Lawrences, some with large estates. There were Tuckers, Van Rensselaers, titled Gabriels with orchards rife with grouse, swales full of woodcock. From this gentry and those who married in arose an impressive array of marvelous shots with a dirth of good dogs, the exception being ones from the few trainers among them, or Brittanies trained by Leon Gordon, a black professional who lived in the community. When invited I would go along to observe recalcitrant brutes let out of their crates like dogs possessed, ignoring basic commands, running amok and even saw one criminal lift its leg on its owner's trousers. I promised myself I would always have a proper shooting dog.

My father had no love for the shooting fraternity. Shot raining on the roof from the surrounding shooting preserve made him apoplectic. To me it was heaven, even the odd pheasant falling on the garage roof. I have seen far worse. It was obvious to me that I would have to seek knowledge of this tantalizing world from someone other than my father.

An exception to the bad dog enigma were the Wilson Lloyd Setters. His son Tom and I were best friends, and his father undertook my education, but I was taught hunting by Nod, a patrician dog deaf and thirteen who would walk a mile to meet us at the school bus during bird season. He would escort us as we carried books and homework back to Tom's home. After the 410s were retrieved from the garage this old dog would take us hunting—grouse, woodcock, pheasant or duck—it made no difference to Nod. However, if we missed twice, he would solemnly trot home to his kennel. Pleading, threats, and biscuits had no effect. This old warrior and his master taught me to never be without a fine dog, and to become the best wing shot I could be. Wilson Lloyd suffered a stroke quite young which left his left side paralyzed. He extended the stock of one of his fine guns and shot one armed, but his heart was not in it; he took his own life. I now have his P grade Parker and, as he did, I always use a necktie to belt my hunting trousers.

Convicted murderers, cops on the beat and I have something in common. If I could have that shot back, those #7½s would never have killed that last drummer on Pea Pond Road.

Woodcock Memoir
by A. Ross Jones
BEDFORD, NEW YORK • SEPTEMBER, 1972

I took up woodcock shooting relatively late in life. But I must say, my initial training could not have been more thorough, nor could my instructors have been more competent. In the middle 1940s, it was not generally known that upper Westchester County had a goodly population of native birds and also benefited from the passage of flight birds at fairly regular intervals during the migration season. But such was the case. For some ten years, until new houses began to spring up in favorite covers, the shooting there was just about as good as any to be had this side of Maine and New Brunswick.

My teachers were Wilson Lloyd, Dave McClure, and Bill Randebrock. Bill is still active in duck blinds and quail covers down south, although he must be nearing eighty. And for all I know, he may still be tramping the woodcock covers. But Wilson and Dave are gone.

Dave McClure was a local plumber who was born and raised in the area and knew all of its covers intimately. He was then in his sixties and carried an old Damascus-barreled, 12-gauge L.C. Smith. But like Ed Hewitt, of whom it was once said that he had the ability to think like a trout, Dave could think like a woodcock and frequently located a bird before the dogs did. One time Dave called through the thick briers and alders of a particularly dense patch of cover we were hunting, "I'm on point!" We didn't understand him, and again he called, "I'm on point!" This time we got the message and hurried over to where he was standing. Sure enough, fixed in his gaze and not more than three feet away was a spot of fresh splatter; and with the help of all our eyes, we finally made out the bird sitting huddled nearby.

Dave had a favorite dictum: "Always hunt the (y)edges." Translated, this meant: Be sure to hunt the edges of all the hedgerows and other spots of cover. And more often than not, it was good advice.

Wilson Lloyd was about my own age and an excellent wing shot. He had the keenest interest in shooting I have ever known. Each year, he would take his two-week vacation during the woodcock season and devote almost every waking moment to it. Keeping a regular diary of his shooting, he could quote from it for any given day for years past – the number of birds flown, the number shot, and the number retrieved. Thus the rest of us could be kept informed as to how the current season was stacking up with other years.

Wilson came by his love of shooting naturally. I remember one of his contemporaries from Rumson, New Jersey, where he was raised, telling me about what a great duck hunter Wilson's father was; and how she remembered one day when her mother, hearing footsteps approaching the front door of their home, peered through the lace curtains near the door and exclaimed, "Oh, here comes old Mr. Lloyd again, bringing us some more of those awful ducks!"

And Wilson himself was not without similarly unappreciative acquaintances. One day he violated the sacred precincts of a heavily posted cover belonging to some friends and picked off several woodcock. Not knowing that the lady of the house was a pillar of the local Audubon Society, Wilson, considerate person that he was, thought it would be a nice gesture to leave off a pair of birds for his unwitting hosts. He rang the doorbell, and when the lady answered, he handed her two very dead and shot-bedraggled woodcock. Without uttering a word of thanks or otherwise, she shrieked "Eeek!" and slammed the door.

Wilson had hunted with Randebrock for many years and from him, I am sure, learned most of what he knew about the sport. Randebrock was not only a better-than-average shot, but also a student of the woodcock, its habit and its habitat. One of the best books ever written on woodcock shooting was by John Alden Knight, and much of its content, I am told, was cribbed from conversations with Randebrock, who also supplied some of the photographs.

By the time I entered the picture, Dave McClure still went along on shoots but, as happens to many of us as we grow older, had lost much of his desire to kill and went along simply for the joy of watching the dogs work and to applaud the good shots made by the rest of us. But Lloyd and Randebrock were as keen as ever. And there existed between them an intense competition to "wipe the eye" of the other. As a consequence, I, the neophyte, found it quite difficult to bag my share of the birds. No sooner was a woodcock flushed or sighted in full flight than the woods were filled with cries of "Mark!" "Mark!" and it then became a case of first-come, first-served. Even though the bird by all rights seemed to be mine to shoot at, it frequently happened that, because of the alacrity of the other two gunners, by the time I had gotten my gun up and off, I found myself shooting at a falling bird. It took me some time to realize that I must always carry my gun at "port arms" — never in one hand only or over my shoulder — if I expected to have a chance at downing the bird. The others were so fast and so accurate that I could never let my attention wander for even a second. To give himself an edge, Lloyd even hunted with his safety off, which gave me an occasional twinge whenever I found him walking behind me.

As a result, it was several seasons before I reached the point where, in the midst of this intense rivalry, I could hold my own. It made me a better wing shot than I could ever have hoped to be otherwise.

Those were happy days. We would take to the covers while the morning dew was still heavy on the brush and would struggle through catbriers and alders the entire morning. Then we'd repair to the Cabin, a roadside bar and grill, for a martini and a large lunch of ham and eggs and home-fried potatoes — that was all they could cook properly — washed down with some ale. Then, after much good conversation and without even a nap, back to the covers until the sun went down and the woodcock getting up wild-flitted by in the gathering dusk like the ghosts they were.

Lloyd and I were attired in much the same fashion as the hunters in A.B. Frost prints, but Randebrock was truly distinctive. Against the early morning chill he wore a much-abused old camel's hair polo coat. Once upon a time, it must have had real class. Now the left sleeve was hanging by only a few threads, having been almost torn off by the clutching briers found in most grouse and woodcock covers.

And the dog work was superlative. In the early years, we had both Randebrock's English Setter, Brownie, of everlasting fame as the subject of "His Last Bird," which appeared in the *Bulletin* several years ago, and Lloyd's English Setter Nod (his litter mates were Wynken and Blynken). I have particularly fond recollections of Nod—so old and slow that he puttered rather than ranged, but so sure and accurate that he rarely missed a bird and never a retrieve. When his bell would stop ringing, Wilson would yell, "Nod's on point!" and all of us would hurry to find him, because we knew that when we did, we also would find a bird.

One day we were hunting a particularly difficult piece of cover, Carrie the Cook's; Carrie cooked for Dave for many years. As we entered the cover, we noticed a two-horse team hitched to a farm wagon that stood in a little dirt road alongside the cover. The teamster was not in sight. After a few minutes, we found ourselves in a patch of catbriers so thick that one could hardly raise his arms—and at that moment, Nod went on point. Wilson stepped in and flushed the bird, which then fell to a volley of our shots. At the sound of the guns, we heard the horses give a frightened neigh, and then there was a tremendous clatter of hoof beats and a screech of wagon wheels from which the handbrake had not been released as the team tore down the dirt road. The driver was on foot behind it screaming "Whoa! Whoa!" for all he was worth. We were all so startled and at the same time so contrite and embarrassed at having caused a runaway that without another word we slunk away as silently as possible to the far side of the cover, intending to make our way back to the car by a roundabout route and thus avoid the teamsters' wrath. We were just about clear of the place when we looked back, and there was Nod, who also undoubtedly had been cowed by what had happened. Slowly, and silently, he was picking his way after us—with a dead woodcock in his mouth!

Most of these covers are gone now. Obliterated by bulldozers and replaced with houses and concrete roads. So-called progress has had its way.

— 19 —

HOLLOWVILLE, NEW YORK • APRIL 2003

Drinking with Dogs

Slick Henderson's . . . unique psychological discovery, the unearthing of mankind's ten stages of drunkenness, which are:
   Witty and Charming
   Rich and Powerful
   Benevolent
   Clairvoyant
   Forget Dinner
   Patriotic
   Crank up the Enola Gay
   Witty and Charming Part II
   Invisible
   Bullet Proof
   The last state . . . almost certain to end a marriage.
            —From *Baja Oklahoma*, by Dan Jenkins

Drinking with Dogs

The night before, at a party of my wife's friends, I had been somewhere between Witty and Charming Part II and Bulletproof when the evening terminated around two A.M. with both vehicles stuck a mile from home at ten below. The following morning I was not in a mood for spousal confrontation.

"If you *ever* drink one of those straight up martinis again, I'm leaving!"

I slowly walked to the liquor cabinet, which was an antique wooden icebox, and took out a shaker and silver spoon. Pouring a proper amount of Gilbey's gin and Italian dry vermouth ratio 4 to 1 in a tulip glass, added a twist . . . I raised my glass to her.

"Cheers, My Dear." And drained it. The marriage limped on for another six months and then dissolved.

Some would say martinis have ruined my life, I do not agree. I still embrace them with the verve of my youth, sometimes with my few friends, but generally at home with my dogs. I am a trainer of hunting dogs—up to four of which live in my house so, though I enjoy solitary drinking, I don't have to drink alone.

Alcohol is not good for dogs, though we hear of alcoholic fraternity house mutts, most of which die young. Their livers aren't beer tolerant. Even if dogs' systems did not reject gin, most smell it and turn their heads away. Unlike twelve steppers, dogs are silent non-drinking companions. I am a mellow, pensive drunk. If I were abusive I would not drink so my dogs need not fear me. Field Champion Panda, an English Springer Spaniel, lost her first owner to a tree and would count my drinks. If I began to mix a fourth one she would leave the room with gravitas. Her opposite was another Spaniel, Tweed IV; there were three others, all liked drunks. Possessed of great bonhomie, he would grin and push me to achieve new personal bests. It was fortunate their lives overlapped. When Panda died Mildred, a Shorthair, took over her temperance role. Until vehicular homicide she was as close to a wife as I have had in twenty-five years. If she had been given thumbs she would have cooked and cleaned.

Currently my entourage is but two Spaniels. Arrow is ambivalent to imbibing but passionate about food. A great competitor in her day, at eight she has lost her girlish figure and is always on a diet. She realizes that the longer the cocktail hour the longer she has to wait for treats and plate licking. She also knows the more cocktails I have the more generous I get. Barney, a youngster whose personality is redolent of his namesake—that large purple creature on TV—sits between my feet and grunts. Tomorrow is his birthday, which, by coincidence, is the same day as Tweed IV, now gone. The dogs will be served canned dog food, which they only get on their birthdays, and I will memorialize Tweed while imbibing martinis. We'll have a high old time.

Years ago a wag named my kennel "Liver's End," which is our registered name to this day.

Think of the advantages of drinking with dogs. They are cheap drinkers content with a full water bowl. They won't take the last drink in your bottle. You do not have to leave home for companionship, exposing yourself to the booze Nazis' wrath by driving home. I have not one living relative and am a semi-hermit content with my own company embellished by dogs. In the extreme I turn down holiday invitations with other people's families to eat a sumptuous feast and get drunk with my dogs. This is not for everyone.

And the dogs prosper from boozy love and indoor dwelling. The abusers I have known as trainers are dry drunks and should not be around kids or dogs. Tweed I, owned in my twenties was the only dog to suffer any damage and it was from my lifestyle as a single ski instructor who owned his own bar. Tweed never

Drinking with Dogs

knew where he would sleep or if. Drinks were spilled on him when he tended bar with me but so were hamburgers. The pace was frantic and the hours long, but he lived to fifteen.

Now I am playing my own fifteenth hole with a regimen that demands an early infusion of gin and an early bedtime. If I am reincarnated, I would like to do so as one of my Spaniels.

"Drinking with Dogs" was submitted to *Modern Drunkard Magazine* (Yes, there really is such a publication; a bimonthly from Denver, to which I subscribe.)

— 20 —

CAPE BRETON ISLAND • JULY 2000

Tree Houses

If there are any lady readers left thumbing these pages, I suggest that they skip this chapter. Not because of raw language or intentional gender slurs; simply put, it will anger even the most understanding of women in this modern age. Why be angry?

A primal urge among men from age five is the exclusion of women from certain activities and organizations. Boys' tree houses are the most extreme early manifestation. To protect male sanctity one need only raise a rope ladder, allowing the boys within privacy to gloat and even throw unpleasant objects at those excluded below. The girls retaliate with their own male-free activities and clubs that men and boys are perfectly content to leave alone. The male equivalent of a tomboy is something entirely different.

At the highest levels women are invading old-boy business networks and sacrosanct clubs. I was a member of the New York University Club when under siege. The club did not buckle without a fierce struggle against feminists, the ACLU, wimpy members and the Tax Department. There was a militant group within the club, of which I was one, who fought to the bitter end. In face of the inevitable most resigned, some who were fifty-year members. As a final defiant act they volunteered to provide the exercise equipment for the new ladies' salon. Imagine the displeasure when these new members opened the doors and found an assortment of brooms, mops and old vacuums ready for use.

The all-male private golf clubs remaining can be counted on one hand; even most men's grills are gone. Aside from the sacred right of deer camp, which will be the last holdout, gentleman's sporting clubs are extinct. I know of one to which a visionary member left an enormous annuity that ceases the day a woman is accepted for membership. Supposedly he had an unhappy marriage.

I came to Atlantic salmon fishing somewhat late in life, having fished trout in every possible location from the Arctic south. For myriad reasons I chose to buy property for a camp in Nova Scotia. The concept of a club evolved during the five years before construction. My mentor for such advice, Mr. Tilt, was in his eighties and a veteran of many of the great camps. Fewer than a dozen men would own miles of pools on such hallowed rivers as the Restigouche, Miramichi, Tobique, Cascapedia and Moisie. His admonishments were few: select the members with care, no women or kids. Mr. Tilt is memorialized on a plaque, our first honorary member. He meant not only no women members, but no women in camp . . . period. The wisdom of this was irrefutable; a camp with women and children is a vacation spot, not a fishing camp. Oh sure, fishing can be done, but the focus is diluted. I wanted no more than a dozen members with succession through their sons, and their sons, and so on. I wrote a very explicit invitation to a select group. A few felt the rules were not right for them or their families, the rest joined. One wife, with whom an incautious husband shared the letter, was miffed, having known me for years. I guess she never really knew me well. The interior of the camp was designed to accommodate up to four, and a charter written, which the politically correct police would burn with the drafter. In effect we had our tree house.

High voices in a fishing or hunting camp bug me. They don't belong there and detract terribly from the ambiance. Author Dana Lamb chronicled in *One Evening* a surprise visit by a guest Duke, with his wife, "the Duchess," to a men's trout camp in the Catskills. The rules had been broken, the magical evening spoiled and with rare vitriol the author suggested that this guest will not again be welcome. Men act differently when women are around, and are more at ease when they are not. It is fashionable these days to poke fun at male bonding. The notion of a group of inepts getting drunk, eating terrible food in abject squalor without a steadying feminine hand is a source of scorn. What is it that women fear? Those experienced men who know will agree that the most elegant food and wine, stimulating conversation and neat orderly surroundings are found in the company of other men . . . in camp. Of course the quality of camp life is only as fine as the quality of the campers. Introduce one woman to the mix, and the entire scene changes. To a lesser degree the addition of a child under fourteen has the same effect. The men become less open with each other. Even the guy who brought her feels the pinch. At the risk of indelicacy, it seems that couples in camp who have not shared intimacy in a year feel obligated to do so in camp, to the mutual embarrassment of all parties as they appear at breakfast sporting feigned afterglow. This motivation to perform in camp is similar to what happens during natural disasters and war. It is all too much.

"What do women want?" Freud cried in frustration and despair, "Sig," I reply, "I have no idea, but it isn't my fishing club, though some don't realize it." Wistfully some of the members' wives inquire about "bending" the rules. Most are good friends who entertain me in their homes. I remain resolute, and I see open relief in their spouse's eyes, sometimes only a flicker.

One day at Seal Pool with Joe, one of our guides, we sat on the bench awaiting our turn in rotation. Impeccably dressed arrived a handsome older couple with Spey rods and their English Setter. It was all too perfect. She sat down and proceeded to chat about the rivers she fished, the flies she tied, the sports she knew from the States. She was an extremely attractive lady. We invited her to take a turn ahead of us as we already had a pass.

When she was out of earshot Joe asked, "Why isn't she home baking cookies?" His wife Roseanne was. I laughed so hard I fell off the bench onto the shingle.

"What's so funny?" said Joe, "I'd say the same to Joan Wulff."

I am no Doctor Laura. Lord knows I've had my own marriage problems and chose to remain a bachelor through thick and thin ever after, but it seems we need more tree houses and more cookies. Certainly what we have now doesn't work very well. A gaggle of angry and unattractive women captured the hearts and minds of their sisters, liberating them but unable to supply direction as to how they fulfill their own lives, let alone the lives of those who marry them or of the children they bear. Member Wilson talks about his last relationship.

"She had an agenda for me of travel and social engagements with strangers that had nothing to do with my agenda of hunting and fishing, which she hated."

He broke the engagement and fled his Texas home to Oregon to get away from her.

I am in camp sedulously avoiding my inner child and woman within. I am alone with two dogs awaiting The Run and the first members who come for it. At peace looking out on the Gulf and Margaree Island, my only regret is that I was not able to do this ten years sooner so that I could have had more of it. I must admit that I really outdid myself in masculine trappings. With the exception of a few nice pieces and generous offerings from members' attics the furnishings are garage sale bought as a lot for $150. The bunks are built in. The camp and all appliances are new. Everywhere are brass signs PIPES OR CIGARS ONLY, EVERY INDULGENCE HAS ITS PRICE. A shelf is built into the stonework above the Franklin stove on which is a 40-ounce Tanqueray bottle off which hang my Marine Corps dog tags awaiting as many of my ashes as it will hold. Fish pictures and memorabilia of members are everywhere with lots of framed photos of me in various stages of youth and decrepitude. A commissioned portrait of Spaniels Tweed I-IV hangs high in the place of honor. And what do you do with your former wife's wedding portrait by Bachrach? Perfect in my room.

The days of private water, angling in ties and killing unlimited numbers of salmon are only memories. But we are doing our best to preserve the most sacred of the traditions right here...in camp!

— 21 —

WATERBURY, VERMONT • APRIL 2000

Same-Sex Union and Dog Ownership

Vermont has been catapulted to worldwide prominence with a historic piece of legislation, so the framers say, signed into law by Governor Dean. Albeit he signed the same sex betrothal law with as little fanfare as possible, fearing backlash in November. But it was difficult to downplay, even though he hid in his office during the signing, afterward mumbling platitudes to the press. Every major network was there, capturing footage of triumphant same-sex couples embracing, to run as feature stories on evening news.

I hope I'm wrong, I don't see any reprisals in November, though polls show the bill highly out of favor with the Vermont voters who elected the legislators to represent them. Some of these lawmakers were bold enough to say they didn't care what their constituents felt, they were going to support what they felt was right. They deserve to be pilloried by the members of the communities who elected them, but I bet those arrogant clowns escape all punishment.

In the mean time, states that do not have laws on the books

defining marriage as "between one man and one woman" are hastening to do so . . . too late. Vermont will lead the way. Once these *causes célèbres* get momentum, the U.S. Constitution itself is swept aside, puny state measures easily repealed. Even the Vermont House attempted to hedge by granting civil union, not marriage licenses. The ink from the Governor's pen was barely dry when it became obvious how long this would last. A matched pair of gravel-voiced lesbian activists who were instrumental in moving matters through the courts referred to the bill as a first step toward marriage, honoring their twenty-seven-year commitment. The old gals seemed nice enough, enjoying handholding on their farm for the cameras.

Vermont's image to this day among the totally uninformed is—conservative, Republican, Yankee? Well not anymore and not since the sixties, when almost as a lark the state elected a Democrat governor. Unheard of. He was a prodigious drinker and party man who was known on at least one occasion to tumble downstairs into a press conference. He was fun, charismatic (never forgot a face or a name) and though he did not bring sweeping change, Vermont as a one-party state was past. Then the hippies and liberals with a mission visited and unfortunately stayed. In the year 2000 our one congressman is an old hippie from Brooklyn, a socialist independent. Our senators are dinosaurs; the Republican switched to independent and is more liberal than the Democrat. The bureaucracy of state support workers for our limousine-liberal governor (from Locust Valley, Long Island) has swollen to double since he came to office. The Republican Party is in such disarray that a joke candidate ran in 1998 for the U.S. Senate, an 80-year-old farmer who did not even vote for himself.

Of course, anyone opposing same sex-marriage is despised and ridiculed as a mean-spirited cad. The press joined the fray, as did children poorly educated in a failed liberal education system, but well indoctrinated in schools that show documentaries like *Heather Has Two Moms*. People are scared.

Okay, they win, but fair is fair. I want to legally marry my German Shorthair, Mildred. Same-sex marriages, why not mixed species? The unisexers state that it is discriminatory not to recognize love and commitment. I love my hunting dog and she loves me unconditionally, which is more than I've had out of marriage and other relationships with humans. Of course, I didn't deserve such devotion, but Mildred neither knows nor cares. Panda, an English Springer Spaniel who shared my life for fifteen years, would have married me at the drop of a hat, and she was an open-field trial champion. She did get cranky and used to leave the room if I mixed a third martini. Divorce? Never? If one thinks a 50 percent divorce rate amongst hetero couples is high, wait until the courts clog with same-sex divorce, in spite of their mantras about commitment.

My dog union is just the tip of the iceberg; all pets should qualify—Mrs. O'Leary and her cow, Tarzan and his favorite ape—the opportunities are endless. My dogs sleep on my bed, not in it and besides, most married couples, for all intents, stop having "meaningful sex" anyway. Those who talk about great home sex are lying. Bill and Hillary stopped having relations a dozen years ago according to his testimony, and they are icons. If I were so inclined I could marry my dog in Vermont and move to a state like Missouri, which has no laws against bestiality, with liberal psychiatrists and their lawyers fighting to keep it so on the basis that it provides relief for psychotics *if the animal is consenting*. These are strange times, mama . . . strange times indeed.

The obvious extension of all this is allowing same-sex marriage to mixed species. To this I answer absolutely not! What is our society, perverted?

Pure, Crass Canine Prejudice
A Response by Peter Miller

I have known Mr. Ross for years. He calls me a flaming liberal and I call him a redneck conservative but I am shocked, absolutely shocked, that Mr. Ross will marry Mildred, a bitch he picked up in Texas a few years ago, and not his stalwart male companion for the last fifteen years, Tweed IV. Tweed is his favorite Springer Spaniel and many times I have caught him kissing the dog. I know Tweed and Mildred share Mr. Ross's bed.

Mr. Ross implies that Mildred could sleep under the covers, if she is so inclined (he didn't mention what Mildred thought of the idea). What kind of marriage does this dog owner propose with Mildred? A nonconsummated platonic marriage? And if that is so, why won't he marry his male companion Tweed, who has been such a faithful companion and a good hunter?

The reason is just plain prejudice. Mr. Ross is against same-sex marriage or mixed species, same-sex civil union. I know his heart lies with Tweed; their love and affection for each other is boundless. Like many conservatives, Mr. Ross follows the politically correct social mantra instead of allowing his libido to have some say in the matter. Mr. Ross is not in the closet, but he is in the doghouse when it comes to canines.

Civil union gives legality to same-sex marriage and as Mr. Ross implies, it can lead to legal dissolution, which is divorce. The lawyers will soon be burnishing their skills in civil union dissolution as they anticipate further financial rewards from the emotionally distressed. But who is going to handle dog-human or other mixed-species dissolution? Will the animal rights people start hiring and training lawyers and putting judges on retainers? You bet your pooch the human won't get a fair shake.

Will there become canine or feline specialists in divorce? And how will the settlement be configured? If the present laws are honored, Mildred, if she divorces Mr. Ross, will own half of his home, bark Mr. Ross out of the premises and show Tweed the door. And to whom will Mildred will the house? And can Mildred or Tweed or any same-sex or hetero-sex mixed-species marriage–civil union partner-husband-wife get restraining orders *if he, she or it is abused by their mate?*

I think, in the case of Mr. Ross, he should be allowed to marry his bitch, Mildred, and enter into civil union with Tweed, and draw up a pre-nuptial agreement between the two dogs for as long as they are allowed to sleep on Mr. Ross's bed.

— 22 —

STEADY BROOK, NEWFOUNDLAND • AUGUST 2000

Travels with Tweed IV

In 1960, the year I graduated from Union College, Icon John Steinbeck took to the road with his standard poodle, Charley, in search of America. He did not find it, and the book was a bit of a potboiler. If you or I had written it we would have had difficulty finding a publisher. *Travels with Charley*, critically acclaimed, sold in the millions vindicating fame over talent.

In the summer, August 2000, I set out with Tweed to find my roots in Newfoundland. To my knowledge I have not one living relative. A comparative score card—Steinbeck and Ross.

	T.R.	J.S.
Fame	Little known	Famous writer
Age	62	58 in 1960
Current status	Alive	Dead
Physical Condition	About average	Above average
Alcohol Consumption	Copious	Copious
Dog Companion	Spaniel, 14 years, Tweed	Poodle, 10 years, Charley
Road Experience	Enormous	Limited
Vehicle	13-year-old wagon 20-year-old trailer, Stonefly III	1960 brand-new GM truck with custom-built camper, Rocinante (Don Quixote's horse)
Roads	Newfoundland 2000	USA 1960

Analysis

Charley's reader finds J.S. is never too comfortable with this self-imposed assignment. A critic once said of Thoreau that he never camped too far from Mrs. Emerson's kitchen. The further J.S. strays from Sag Harbour, Long Island, not in miles but culture, the less comfortable he becomes. He gets physically and mentally lost and if confronted with a problem; without ready aid he could be in trouble. His dog, except for a flare-up of prostatitis, seems more adaptable, even though he is a much-pampered French poodle, for heaven's sake. J.S. never really understands his subjects though some are wonderful; an itinerate traveling actor stands out. Most portraits are as shallow as his understanding of regionality. Twice his wife flew out to meet him, breaking fragile momentum. He dispenses whiskey and very good company to his interviewees. There is the duty 1960s segregation piece with white villains and black heroes. Shabby stuff because he never really left Sag Harbour. Enough Steinbeck bashing! I loved all of his books, especially *Red Pony*.

Countless years of my life have been spent towing and driving camping vehicles, and I have earned my living out of them. I can fix them poorly when they break, and panic never sets in when they quit. Some who have journeyed with me feel in constant peril, oft-times justified. When things go wrong there is always a solution. Put me in a boat and positions are reversed. Being a hermit of choice, a dog companion is plenty and I cannot conjure a single old girlfriend who would fly in to break up my journey.

Stonefly I, a motor home named for that slow and inept flying insect that all trout fishermen love, is stationary now. I dwell in it to train dogs in rural New York. It will start and would run if need be. It is a wreck that owes me nothing. Stoner II was a sister ship owned by fishing pals still living; the vehicle is deceased.

Stoner III is a Layton trailer circa 1975, purchased by a surrogate godson who thought to emulate my lifestyle. It ended up at my Vermont house. I towed her to Cape Breton, Nova Scotia, to live in while a camp was under construction for three years. It has since been a storage shed and refuge to mice and squirrels. It will not be returning from Newfoundland. The highest recorded wind in recent history blew it over a bank, popping seams and breaking windows that are now repaired with adhesive and metallic duct tape. But the heavy metal frame is intact, the roof sound.

My summer schedule is subject to the whims of members who wish to come to camp. August salmon fishing is generally low-water doldrums time and year 2000 is no exception. Tweed and I have three weeks before we must return to camp. Two days are spent cleaning Stoner III and freeing a frozen wheel bearing. We are packed and ready for a quest to find my family lineage in Newfoundland.

"A journey always begins with the littlest step," says the adage. The hitch bottoms out at the end of the driveway. Clearance is about three inches off the road. The tow vehicle is the last in a succession of giant, nine-passenger GM wagons. I buy these with low mileage because they suit my lifestyle and the massive amount of dogs and *impedimentia* that I haul about. Maintained on a rigid schedule, they reward me with 250,000 miles of faithful use. This will be the last one I will find.

Service at the Cap Lemoine garage in Nova Scotia reveals the worn trailer wheel bearing will have to be replaced in Newfoundland along with heavy-duty shocks for the Olds.

My traveling companion, Tweed IV, is near the end. At fourteen he weaves like a drunk because of bad knees. Like many professional athletes, legion field trials took the ligaments out and arthritis set in. Sometimes he falls over but gets right back up with an "it's nothing" look. He is the toughest animal I have known. He jumps out of and into things, collapses and struggles on, always in good spirits. If still here I will give him some light hunts this autumn. He cannot hear the gun but marks with excellent eyes and retrieves to hand with gums and a few teeth. We have an intricate communication system of hand signals, body language and nudges that he often ignores. Tweed is friendly but lurching toward people his smiling bonhomie is sometimes misinterpreted as dementia or rabies. Their loss.

I think he is starting to imagine noises so his behavior is ofttimes weird. His cooling system is shutting down, so he pants incessantly in the heat and drinks gallons of water. He is a road warrior of numberless battles and we suit each other. He is still a handsome guy with little graying of muzzle, a big blocky Springer of the Saighton line in the 1980s that won everything there was to win.

My mother's maiden name was Winter. Her father's family emigrated from St. John's, Newfoundland. There were at least five brothers and one mad sister. The family business was export and import: coffee, sugar and rum. My grandfather and grandmother met through her brother at Princeton University, where he was friends with her future husband. Katherine was erudite Southern and used to speak deprecatingly about a visit from her in-laws as "a run of cod." I remember them ever so slightly as outgoing, earthy and more than a touch eccentric. Except for my grandfather, the eldest, who was taciturn.

Newfoundlanders I have met are extremely friendly and love a drink and a party. A word about the national drink, Screech Rum, for which I hold an inbred fondness. It is made in Jamaica, traded for salt fish, and bottled in St. John's. It has a narcotic effect similar to mescal but without the worm. Screech and strong Black Horse beer are the foundation of some high times. Newfies are the subject of countless jokes, most in good fun and frequently at their own expense: "What's a dope ring? Five Newfies standing in a circle." "How does a Newfie count fish? One, two and another one and another one . . ." etc. Their toughness is legendary; descendents of Devon, England ,fishermen who jumped ship, they were forbidden to homestead, so they frequently paired with native women from a tribe they eventually exterminated, neither a proud nor an openly discussed part of Canadian history. Of course, Newfoundland did not become a part of Canada until 1949. Newfoundlander regiments were feared by the Hun for their noisy and murderous charges. Could Screech have been involved? Independent and irreverent to this day, they distrust and ridicule all government—a noble trait.

Newfoundlanders are famously resourceful. Unemployment rates are *reported* by government survey at over 20 percent but these people do well with little, and they do it laughing.

Accessible only by air or boat, the ferry dock in North Sidney, Nova Scotia, is only seventy-five miles from my camp. To me the journey to a destination is as important as what goes on when I get there. From the soft magical light of the Margaree Valley, Tweed and I pass through hill country past two other scheduled salmon rivers, now almost dry. On to Baddeck on the Bras D'Or Lakes where Alexander Bell spent his summers, and home to a world-class golf course. A must luncheon stop for fish cakes at the Telegraph Hill House. The turn-of-the-century dining room is staffed by turn-of-the-century waitresses. An impromptu piano concert is given by a diner, haunting Celtic tunes. I thank her and get a shy smile. The lobby and common rooms are an eclectic mix of *Silver Dart* memorabilia, Nova Scotia's *Kitty Hawk;* clippings including a visit by a Japanese prince and a shrine to Princess Di. A gas fire burns winter and summer. Between Baddeck and Sydney looms Kelly Mountain, which affords views of the inland sea comprised of the Bras D'Or Lakes. Dragging Stoner up the climb in this day's extreme heat threatens a boilover. Just as we begin our ascent the sun goes in and we crest without incident. With hours to spend before the midnight boat, we lumber on to Sydney. To other Cape Bretoners this steel and mining city is an enigma. Tales are told of anglers from here conking salmon on the head regardless of mandatory catch-and-release and throwing them in the trunk to take home. Sydney is home to a unique choral group of miners who perform thirty-strong in helmets equipped with lights, "Men of the Deep" is their stage name. We pass the ancestral home of the McCurdy family, one of which was pilot of the *Dart*. Also ancestral home to Doctor Dave, Spaniel breeder and competitor, still active at almost ninety with the Saighton line from Wales, which he imported thirty-five years ago. Tweed lowers his head in reverence as we pass the former kennel and what is now a bed-and-breakfast, the Rocking Horse. And on to the casino, which has a larger counterpart in Halifax. The endeavour is a Rabelaisian project involving Sheraton International, the province, and the First Nation. For some undisclosed reason dice games are banned, but a combination of blackjack, roulette and the slots finances a portion of our trip. Supper and two surprisingly good Tanqueray martinis and we depart for the boat bottoming out and mushrooming the pole that cranks up Stoner. We will complete the job on the ferry ramp, fortunately only cosmetic. Ample time for a stop at the provincial liquor store. No bottled alcohol is sold except by this monopoly. At least in Newfoundland you can purchase your beer from private enterprise. Astoundingly the

Nova Scotia Liquor Commission is not profitable, and there is discussion of closing the stores and reverting to private distribution. The commission controls the prices, a cheap bottle of vodka is $21, yet they cannot show a profit, another sad testimony to government efficiency.

The attractive blond girl checking out my bottle of Screech was interrupted by an apoplectic seafaring drunk from central casting. "Aye Girlie, I hear old Kenny is in hospital. I'm going to buy him a present, what's his pizen (poison)?"

"Oh, pretty much anything I guess," she replied.

"I'll get him some o' that peppermint schnapps." The old salt left the counter to pick up his gift.

"His friend isn't too picky; he's in hospital from imbibing windshield-wash antifreeze," said the girl.

Expecting to be first car in line on arrival I was surprised to find a party atmosphere with over a hundred vehicles there already. Passengers are drinking, visiting and having a *ceilidh*, Gaelic for kitchen party. There are pipes and a violinist in the group. The bottle I brought is severely dented. People come over to pet Tweed and chat. A properly dressed and garrulous elderly Newfoundlander stops by. He knows of my family, Winter, in St. John's and states, "They were a step up so I don't know them socially." Clinton's quest for a legacy has traveled far. "I think in spite of his troubles he's been a great president for you folks, done a lot of good . . . You going to vote for Gore?" I abstain from comment.

We board and against boat regulations Tweed, the Screech remnants, and I retire in Stoner for the night. Bombarded by endless announcements in English and, of course, the compulsory unaccented French, we sleep until disembarkation. Newfoundland is six hours from North Sydney, including the half-hour time change. I jump out in my socks mildly hung over, and drive up the ramp, catching the jack pole again, into a dull day dawning in Port aux Basques. Friends excoriate me when I seriously rate November my favorite month. Although it is August, the brooding sky and crisply outlined hills of Newfoundland dropping into a gray sea seems late autumn. A Scottish mist hangs in the air and I love it all along the TransCanada towards Corner Brook on the southwest coast. We make multiple stops and Tweed frolicks like a pup while I quaff a morning Black Horse. This weather is our legacy.

The True Northwoods begins where the corn ends and the wood scent begins. When growing up I remember the clean smell of pine and deep woods in all of northern New England and the Adirondacks. Possibly my olfactory sense is now so jaded from booze and cigars that I can only enjoy it in concentrated Newfoundland doses.

Around lunchtime as we were stretching a three-hour drive into a jaunt, we spied a gas stop, almost $3 U.S. per gallon, and a modest restaurant. I wept for joy seeing cod cheeks and tongues on the menu. They are like deep-fried scallops; the tongues have little bags of jelly at the tips.

My grandmother made few concessions to the ubiquitous cod, but one was to allow my grandfather to prepare fish and brewis for alternate Sunday breakfasts after church. All their money was gone by that time, so grandfather did not fear offending the kitchen staff. Brewis is stale bread or hard biscuits soaked with salt-cod chunks for a week, steamed in a double boiler and served with butter or lard and lots of black pepper. My grandmother would take to her bed with the vapors when this was served and so do my camp brethern when I try to feed brewis to them. I love all things cod.

I retired to Stoner for a read and a kip, awoke at 5 P.M. and returned to the Hungry Bear Restaurant for a dinner portion of cod cheeks. My wee dark-haired waitress shyly says, "Oh, you enjoy those so much, it makes me hungry just to watch." I give her one to devour behind the door out of sight of the cook. Everyone is genuinely delighted you have come from "away," want to know where you are going and all about you. It isn't an act.

A side note, Vermont license plates are a great asset. Universally, throughout the U.S. and Canada, they are seen as the least threatening and most welcome. As our current politics and "new" Vermonters become better known this will change. A popular but unheeded bumper sticker in our state is "Enjoy Your Visit." I always play my advantage by carrying a gallon of maple syrup, which I dispense for favors given, hunting and fishing rights granted. Conversely, most threatening and least welcome are from New Jersey in the east, California in the west, with Florida in the south and Ontario in Canada.

So I asked to camp in the back lot with a few truckers driving Day and Ross orange semis and stayed for breakfast, a huge meal extremely cheap. The menu was bear themed as was the décor. On each table was a rating sheet similar to the ones in your room in motel chains. The difference being that here they were heeded. The entire staff would be devastated by a poor score, so I honestly gave the highest mark in each category, stuffed the form in the box, left a generous tip and drove off toward Corner Brook.

A fishing friend has a real-estate venture at Marble Mountain Ski Area. He will be here in two days, so I have time to explore. The Humber is a famous salmon river known for big fall fish, some in the forty-pound class. The river water level is controlled from Deer Lake, a relatively short swim and where the big fish spawn. We drove along it through a narrow granite pass, and it is gloriously dark and deep down here close to the sea. Experience has taught me ski area parking lots are fine for a stop-over. No one complains and there is little summer traffic. From what I can see the mountain has some steep, though it would be a bump even by Vermont standards. What it has is a natural snowfall that Vermont areas would give up a thousand feet elevation for. Marble is a government project and one wonders how well it does in ticket sales. The lift is a modern detachable quad named the Governor. The base lodge is dramatic architecture with slanted high windows and enormous treated wood decks, no doubt very costly construction.

I made an appointment with Wade's garage for Monday repairs. There is a washroom in the lodge, though for some undetected reason only hot water comes out of the taps or into the commodes. And there is a pond for Tweed to swim in. Bliss! On the shore is a heritage tree, which talented carvers have transformed into a shrine of Newfoundland history with a donation box and guestbook in a tiny adjoining building. A tour bus from Ontario stopped around noon. The passengers power milled about and took photographs. Still on schedule, the skiers' shuttle bus stops, but no one gets on or off. Tourist traffic is light in the gift shop.

The high point Sunday for me and quite a few visitors was to be a lift ride to the top. The chair is advertised as offering rides weekends July and August but was broken and awaiting a part. Maybe next weekend I was told, if I could come back. I am sure the view of the river, bay and Blow Me Down (Blomidon) Mountains would be well worth the ticket. Not too long ago Tweed and I would have hiked up. No longer. That evening we hiked to Steady Brook Falls. Sheer guts got Tweed there and back.

The remaining activity is a golf driving range up the beginners slope. A first! Though I once hit floating balls into a snow-making pond. Business was brisk, though right-handed clubs were in short supply. "They break all the clubs; they think they are hockey sticks," said the pleasant blond lady in charge. I told her I had played for over fifty years breaking but one club. "Come see, then" and we went to the back room to view boxes of twisted shafts and cracked heads. Impressed, I settled for a lady's five iron, rental fee—one dollar. "He tried to get three but no one would pay it," said the lady. "I beg for more clubs but he says it's the end of the season (August 12th?), and he's not sure he'll do it again next year." From this I inferred he leased the driving range from the government. It seemed a perfect match. I hit six balls and retreated to Stoner for beer and a kip.

Monday is Stoner Repair Day and I show up for my 9:30 appointment. Parts are ordered and at 10:30 Wade starts work. Changing bearings is a dirty job, but he gets right into it and replaces the rear car shocks as well in about an hour. "Did you haul this thing all the way from Vermont?" "Yes, in stages over about five years, but it's not leaving Newfoundland. I'm going to sell it for two hundred bucks."

"I'll buy her for two hundred bucks, use her in the woods. Drop her off when you're ready to go." With that problem solved and Stoner riding a full inch higher and stiffer we leave. Two miles down the road and a steep hill I hear a horn and see flashing headlights. We stop and the very large lady who commands the front desk gets out of the garage truck carrying the briefcase I left behind. My thanks are profuse. "Didn't want to think of you all the way up the Northern Arm finding you left this. Have a nice trip, my dear. See you when you come back down through."

The plan was to stop in at my friend's condominium project, see him briefly and then go to Gros Morne Park for a week. We provisioned at Deer Lake. The lady at checkout asked where I had come from and I told her over from Cape Breton.

"Oh, my darling!" she says, "Cape Bretoners and Newfies are the finest people on earth, the rest of the world just don't know it yet."

Always expect the unexpected in Newfoundland. A few miles outside the town I see an "Insectarium." It is what it says, and is the only one in Canada, maybe the world. It is housed in a new building, admission six dollars and fabulous, right from the gold scarab beetle in its own case valued at $1,000 or more to the working beehive glass enclosed and vented to the outdoors. I spent two hours fascinated by the exhibits, many of them live. That was the day's pinnacle. As we approached the park the rivers got drier. The Humber, which runs out of Deer Lake is fine. My visions of roadside trout fishing are dashed when I encounter a warden who informed me all the rivers were closed in this part of the park. I am immediately illegal with my cased 16 gauge in Stoner. Almost every tree has a sign warning against gun possession in a national park—the paranoia heralding the draconian gun-control bill soon to be law and eventual confiscation. I drove through the solemn tablelands to Trout River, a mere trickle.

Having spent years in the American West and the East's own White Mountains, mere scenery is not enough for me. So I returned to base and the use of my pal's four bedroom condo for the balance of the week. No outports for us; right back to Mrs. Emerson's kitchen and the company of Harvey Bishop, fishing guide, sixty-eight years old and an intense angler with a well-rounded gut. His hazel eyes and sharp, expressive features betray a humorous soul. Harvey has been in more businesses in the Humber Valley than you can count—trucking, cabins proprietor, mechanic, contractor doing his own electrical and plumbing, certified ski instructor. Officially retired he is head mountain greeter in winter, fishing guide when he wants to be.

"What's the best time of your life?"

"Now."

His house is one hundred yards from the river. Harvey's boat is metal utilitarian with plenty of motor. He fishes every day, often with his buddy Craig, who is much younger.

"I ruined his life when I taught him to fish; he's as bad as me."

Earlier in the summer Craig has taken a thirty-five pound salmon. "Craig won't sit down in the boat, always looking for fish."

He hacks at Craig continuously.

"Drop the anchor on the white rock, not next to it."

How they found this rock is miraculous, as it is the size of a bowling ball in the middle of big water.

The drops are crucial, local knowledge the key. Successive drops are made to the end of two hundred feet of line. It is a treat to watch Harvey's facial changes during his cast or mine; from delight, expectation, grimace to perplexity.

"Lord Jesus, look at that cast; there has to be a salmon."

Colin Montgomery, following an errant golf shot, shows less expression than Harvey does with every cast. Like all fine salmon anglers he never takes his eye off the fly. His moves in the boat are slow and precise, he has never learned to swim. He and I share a seat and one rod in the stern, sitting on the sole remaining plank from a long sunk schooner that happens to fit over the gunnels.

The water is perfect, everything just right, but I am two weeks late, and there are few fish. We cover all the best spots. As happens to me all too often my attention starts to wander, I start telling jokes and pay less attention to the task at hand. It's too much for Harvey.

"Lord Jesus, give me that #&*_! Rod! I can't stand to watch you no more!" Universal laughter. At noon Craig and Harvey are out of smokes, and we head in. Harvey has ceremonial duties at the wedding of a couple he introduced in his role as Mountain Ambassador. The event takes place in the base lodge.

"Craig and I aren't done yet; we'll have a few more salmon before the finish."

On parting we trade dates. He has an annual goose hunt on Prince Edward Island that coincides with a trip I take to a river for a late fall run. We could overlap.

"I feel I've known you all my life, me son."

I wish we had.

Sunday morning we drop off Stoner III with its new owner whose partner says Wade went to a wedding yesterday and won't make it in today. Though he knew nothing of the deal he takes $200 out of the cash drawer and pays me on the spot.

"She'll be a heck of a rabbit catcher," those looking over Stoner repeat several times. I have no idea what that means relative to an old trailer, but there are many Newfoundland expressions which seem obtuse to off-islanders. "Me Trout" as a term of endearment is another.

Something lurks in the Newfoundland soil, made obvious by the serious checkpoint when leaving the island, potatoes may be the culprit because you are asked if you have any. You are then passed through a free car wash and vacuuming station housed in a very permanent building redolent of a major customs crossing. I have learned never to ask questions of even the lowliest bureaucrat—so we passed on.

Tweed, trained on the common street pigeon, showed some of the aggression that triggered his leap as a puppy through a slightly opened window into traffic on Montreal's Ste. Catherine Street at rush hour. He had spotted some pigeons. Fourteen years later he attempts a similar feat at the flock on the ferry dock and has to be moved to his crate. At forty knots, the German-built ferry makes the crossing in under three hours, but it was too hot for Tweed below decks. He was in extremis when I came below to disembark. Another hour and my companion would have been dead. I poured water out of a bottle on to his head and aorta and got him quickly to a swim, reviving him completely.

Reflecting: Tweed and I accomplished little of what we set out to do. We only scratched the surface of The Rock in two weeks. The plan is to resume next summer if we both are able.

Addendum

Alas, Tweed did not make it, but I have found a home on the Humber fishing with Harvey as long as we can.

— 23 —

Steady Brook, Newfoundland • August 2001

The Duck in the Fireplace

Harvey guided me onto a whale of a salmon, thirty pounds or more. We revived her from the beach, receiving honks of approval from truckers on the TransCanada, sending her on her spawning mission up the Humber to Deer Lake.

That evening the Screech Rum, a potent tongue oil, and the designated grilse of honor in a tarragon mustard and lemon sauce prompted some stories.

Bob told one that took place in Donald Trump's palatial office. A black man sporting an Indian headdress was claiming First Nation status for his Long Island tribe and was seeking financing for a proposed casino. Trump, without a flicker of a smile asks, "Chief, what do you call yourself when not using your ceremonial title?"

"Ah be Ricky Pearce."

Not to be outdone by a fancy attorney from Boston, Harvey lets fly.

"I was getting ready to leave for some June trouting with me buddy, Craig, a few hooses down from me. The wife says, 'Harv, there's a flutterin' against the flue in the chimney.'

"'I'm running late and can't be bothered with it. It's probably just a bat.' And I grab my gear and I leaves. In a leedle while Shirly comes runnin' down and singin' out, 'Harv, you got to come home right away, there's a duck in the fireplace. It's a big one too!'

"Well, I runs back to the hoose and sticks me head in and there is a wood duck covered with soot lookin' back at me. All I can see is two white eyes. I put on my winter gloves so I won't get bit. Now the wife and daughter are runnin' around in a panic afraid the thing will get loose in the room and ruin the curtains and carpet. So we assemble all hands, them two holdin' a blanket over me and fireplace. I grab the duck and get out the front door with the thing squawkin' its head off. By this time the commotion has spread through the neighborhood, and everybody and his dog is standin' on me lawn for the show. Of course, I have to have pictures taken of me and that duck for the grandchildren. I'm afraid he won't be able to fly because of the soot on his wings and a dog might get him, so I crosses the road to the river and throws him in the air. Well, Lord Jesus, I watch him fly all the way across and land. Last time I saw him he was cleanin' his feathers with his bill. That's a true story."

The Double Lottery

I chime in, "There's ten times the chance of getting a duck in your fireplace as winning the lottery, twice in a year; one the good kind and one the bad. Fraser lived over to Pleasant Bay and ran a trash collection business in that part of Cape Breton. He was a nice man with a young family and one of the worst left-handed slices I ever saw on a golf course. Well, he won the Maritime Lottery—around two million tax-free. His first action was to rent a floor in the Sheraton so all his family and friends could be there in Halifax when he received his check. Then he went home, built a fine house and gave away a bunch of new cars. I saw him for a time on his trash collection truck, but he soon turned that business over to a relative. After that I saw him more often on the golf course. Not even all that money had done away with the slice. That winter he was out for rabbits. The best reconstruction of events is he slipped on some ice, flew up in the air, lost control of the gun, which flew up as well and landed in front of him. It went off and blew away his stomach. He died right there and was found some hours later when he didn't show up for his supper. Folks calculated the odds of this accident about the same as the lottery he won."

Harvey spun another one about feeding a bunch of his buddies their own gloves disguised as squid stew in retaliation for an earlier prank they played on him on an ice fishing outing. It's a true story.

The Screech gone, I am left to ruminate; landing a thirty-pound Atlantic salmon is just about like winning the lottery. A month later my best pointer, Mildred, was killed on the road. Wish I could give back the salmon for her.

— 24 —

Moscow, Vermont • June 1976

The Great Vermont Capon Hunt

Any who maintain that roosters crow only at dawn should trade places with me for a day. Two enormous, white-feathered monsters, the survivors of a large flock, bray their challenge all day and all night. It's either them or me, winner takes all.

Divorced three years ago, I took up interim residence, only to be for a few months, in a bizarre cabin belonging to my friend Marvin. He built, with the help of me and others, a perfect red clay tennis court. He then found an abandoned structure, that, in the defunct past, had served as a cabin at a kid's camp. Marvin moved it in its entirety to be our tennis house and my home. Taller than it is wide, it has been best described as a referee's chair that someone enclosed. I am comfortable, sort of, the rent is cheap, as it should be, and I make a token income from tennis lessons. I will not be moving soon. Back to the roosters. Marvin surrounds himself periodically with domestic animals tethered to dysfunctional personalities. There was Freda the fun hog whose last act of defiance was to escape onto the clay court, evading with surprising skill Marvin's frenzied efforts to catch her. In a

Herculean display of strength and adrenalin Marvin pitched her over the fence, but not until she had left little cloven holes the entire length and breadth of the court. Only after trapping herself by sticking her head through the rotten net was she captured. Any hopes she might have had for long life were snuffed shortly thereafter.

There have been vicious ponies, omnivorous auto-climbing goats, the odd diarrhetic duck, all presided over by Murtaugh, a pony-sized Irish Wolfhound with car-crushed hindquarters and a sweet but timid demeanor. Raising caponized chickens seemed a harmless enough plan. Out of the two-dozen-plus chicks grew twenty-three eunuch roosters and three hens, which the chicken sexer must have misdiagnosed.

All went well at first with the capons gaining five pounds in a surprisingly short time. I was named official executioner, as Marvin was busy becoming the ordained minister of the Church of the Whispering Pines to achieve tax-free status for himself and his property. Though I don't relish avian execution I have had plenty of practice afield in autumn with gun and dog. A machete and a block work fine, and the neighborhood urchins like to watch the show with the ritual blood spurting as the headless roosters run in circles. I could probably collect admission.

Though not particularly possessed of flavor they were tender and luxuriously greasy, at least the first ten. All of a sudden the remaining birds were ten pounds, tough and hard to pluck. They were not birds eager to approach the block, and were known to gore the knacker—me—with talons and beaks honed like those of eagles.

Five of them wintered over, and they took on a weird appearance and behavior, that could have freaked out Stephen King. They became turkey-sized behemoths of fearsome aspect and aggression, attacking even those brave enough to enter the pen in which they are housed to give them corn. Why Marvin puts up with them is anyone's guess. Mine is that he shares an odd kinship. One of these mutants pecked a bloody hole in Marvin's father's ankle. The gentleman retaliated by striking a crushing blow with a pot containing the feed on the bird's granite skull —"hard enough to drop a man, but not hard enough to bother that damn chicken." Feeding was officially suspended. The poor hens among them have been slowly cannibalized.

Could whatever process used to caponize these creatures have reversed itself, creating a super rooster? These things have perfected limited flight and the constant crowing is indicative of some psychological aberration. Marvin's solution: "You deal with 'em."

I located a farm lady, who was delighted with the opportunity to turn them into chicken potpies on a 50/50 basis. I hoped she had a big enough pot and the patience to boil until tender.

Execution should be a simple matter—firing squad. Priding myself on giving them sporting odds I decided upon a 410. I released them all at once and went indoors for what I felt to be an appropriate amount of time. Of course my Spaniels are terrified of these harpies and will be of no use. The first two roosters are easy and quickly succumb to number fours. Yes, I am ashamed to say, I shot them on the ground. The other three, no fools they, ran around the barn. I reversed direction and met them head on, a terrifying prospect. All three fly downhill into the swamp below, the last one crashing through tree branches like a fallen pterodactyl, shot on the wing.

The last two are lurking in the swamp, crowing their defiance and eating God knows what. The 410 has been replaced by a 12 bore in case I have to deflect a charge. With reptilian eyes I glare into the swamp. If I don't return tell my dogs I loved them.

— 25 —

Cape Breton Island • July 2002

Three Camps Plus One

Blessed in life to visit some of the great fishing camps, I harbor no illusions about Rossfalloon, the one I opened in 1997 on Cape Breton's Gulf Shore. Some of the requisites for greatness are in place—a congenial membership, colorful local guides: Joe, Robert, and Rene are Acadians and members of the vast families whose surnames dominate the region. Ask them if they are related to another of the same name and the answer is "Yes, but way back." However, though the view of the sea is spectacular, with surf breaking on the rocks below, we do not own salmon water. We also have no history past the opening log entry five years ago. In short, we do not qualify for the big league.

My recollections of visits at age twelve and thirteen to the Adirondack League Club are too fuzzy to relate. I remember dark wood and stone camps and wonderful indigenous guide boats on a vast private lake. There was a central club building with the scent of blue-blood exclusivity. The camp and lake were nestled within a network of outlying ponds and streams with rough cabins on thousands of acres owned by the Club.

The three private camps I describe here are very different, yet all have the qualities necessary to make them special.

The Gold Miner's Camp on California's Yuba River was owned by two families. They took over an active mining lease in the early fifties and turned the miner's shack into a comfortable fishing camp without compromising the rusticity. Some felt the outhouse a bit too authentic, so they seldom returned. There was no commercial power or generator, just gaslights. It was not an easy camp to run, but there was always a ready labor source in the many kids and their friends. Fred's mother, Betty-Winn, despised idleness. In a stentorian, cigarette baritone she would exhort us all to "DO SOMETHING." The structure which was never intended as a permanent dwelling, required neverending repairs just to stay even. Wood needed to be cut and stored and an eroding shoreline had to be reinforced and stabilized. The only access to the camp for people and supplies was *The Flying Dutchman* from the road across the river. It was a conveyance, hung from a cable above what was oft-times a raging torrent, powered by human muscle. The camp log tells of a series of natural disasters involving spring floods, pest invasions, break-ins and all the ravages of a winter of enormous Sierra snowfall. Mr. Butts was the caretaker in the off-months, and it was obvious that without his ministrations the battle against nature would end in ruin. I never met him, as he seldom stopped by when the camp was occupied, though a typical camp entry read, "Mr. Butts exterminated the porcupines that moved in over the winter and has replaced the siding they ate. He reported that the outhouse roof had to be replaced after the snow collapsed it during the record snows of '58. He also spliced the cable on the *Dutchman,* which was ready to let go and take us all with it."

As college students, Fred and I often made supply trips from suburban San Francisco in an open, World War II jeep that belonged to the camp. Of course, we did the bare minimum, opting for the local saloons and runs to Nevada casinos, sleeping late and fishing for trout. Yelled at for our sloth, we would affect remorse totally unfelt.

Even in the fifties and sixties the fishing was only fair. The Yuba is not a large river and the boulder-strewn rapids do not lend themselves to hatching and holding big rainbows. Betty-Winn, a fiery redhead who grew up fishing Wisconsin's Brule, was the finest lady angler I have known and very competitive. Though a sixteen-incher was a whale in that stream, she recorded some impressive numbers over some forty years, always besting her men. Her weapons—hellgrammites artificial and real.

The log is now in the elegant camp Fred built up the canyon from the old one. Which brings us to the sad demise of the Gold Miner's Camp. The national park system, the forest rangers and environmentalists combined forces to get rid of it. The vagaries of a gold mining lease made futile the legal battles that Fred waged against this government juggernaut, and the camp is no more. From the high bank where the *Flying Dutchman* was chained there is no evidence that a camp ever existed. Betty-Winn and Mr. Butts are gone as well.

Ile Bature is a private island in the middle of the St. Lawrence River below Quebec City. It is approximately seven miles from either shore, and was a King's Grant made around 1910 to a Canadian family with a stipulation that a portion of the camp be unlocked and provisioned for shipwreck victims. This is a valid concern, as this section of the river is inhospitable with enormous tides, devilish currents and chop from almost constant winds. The island is flat with a slight rise in the center on which the family constructed an elegant camp with four private bedrooms, a formal dining room and main room each with a massive stone fireplace. In the back are the guide and servant quarters. Whether the baths were added later after generators were invented is a question; probably the staff drew and hauled water from the dug well. Through the first half of the century the place was frequently visited. From log entries the use was not just for waterfowl hunting but general vacationing in the summer. Trees were planted around the dwelling (the rest of the island is barren) and at one point a landing strip was put in.

Interest waned with the generation of children after 1950. Though they used it as a hunting camp the copious maintenance required was reduced to the bare minimum to keep the house standing and it was only a matter of time before it was sold or fell to ruin. Just in time an unlikely savior married a daughter. Mogy was from Utah, couldn't swim a stroke, but was a finish carpenter and an ardent waterfowler. The marriage did not hold, however, his love affair and stewardship of the island has lasted forty years. The family was more than willing to turn all the headaches over and allow him to run it as a semi-commercial operation during duck and goose season. What few skills Mogy did not have his friends from Vermont could supply in return for hunts. Over the years the downslide was reversed and improvements made. New roofs, shingles and power plant were only a few of them. Specialized vehicles were moved from shore in pieces and reassembled with oversize tires, and platforms were mounted to carry hunters and gear.

Relations with locals on the mainland had to be reestablished. Palms in the government required frequent grease to allow what was really an illegal American outfitting operation to exist in an often hostile Quebec environment. Mogy, who spoke not one word of French, managed to get along in an area of the province in which almost no English is spoken.

Initially and for many years cooks and guides came over for the hunts as they had in the past. The most important was an adored and unflappable lady who chefed for years, and then retired, unwilling to risk the crossing after two guides drowned. With her gone it became easier to self-manage. I was there at least five times and there was never a shortage of talent on the hunt or in the kitchen when this change was made.

The surface of the island is green mud and shale. Because it is flat the twenty-foot tides contract it to a few hundred yards around the house from several miles at low. There were a few blinds set up but it was more productive to dress in green and stay mobile. A sign at the door admonished "Be a rock." At my current age I could not possibly hunt it right, carrying all gear and decoys through the muck, chasing or retreating from the tide as we set up decoys. A typical hunt: after breakfast and paired off, we check wind and tides anticipated for the day. We gather around Mogy and the VW-powered carryall. The wind is from the southwest and Travis and I elect to walk into it and the outgoing tide. Hugh and John go with Mogy on the vehicle to the other end of the island. We all carry a modest lunch as we won't be back until late afternoon. The limits are generous and the species available as part of a bag rule out an early return. Over the years I have counted four species of geese, including Blue and Ross, all three teal, the usual puddleducks, including gadwall, the odd pintail and even a shoveler. There are four species of divers and, of course, unwelcome mergansers of all types. Mogy has the only dog, a reliable but low-key goose blind companion. Dogs are not necessary and at high risk. The geese are shot over land and the ducks are taken in wader depth off the shoreline. The horror of watching one of my Spaniels chasing a cripple swimming with a following tide into the distance is avoided by just leaving them home.

Our first stop is a set of snowy shells put out the night before. snow geese migrate throughout the day: the awesome sight of thousands of these coming over the hills along the north shore and parachuting slowly down with the attendant calling quickens the pulse. These birds will remain in the area for several weeks or more, resting and refueling on the lush moss and grasses unless driven out by a violent norther. The day is gray and dry with steady but manageable wind. It also is to be one of those rare days when everything will go right.

I hear them before I see them, a flock of the resident Canadas slide low over the camp to a small saltwater pond formed by indented rock.

"Travis, just sit behind that boulder and I'll get on the other side!" I give a couple of grunts on the call.

"They aren't even going to circle; they're going to come right in." Almost too easy, they are thirty yards out with wings cupped. Four shots and three geese are stashed behind the boulder to pick up later and the hunt has not officially begun.

At the snowy set we get similar treatment. A flock of forty circle once and pass right over the top of us. Travis, who has heard how difficult these birds are to fool, is amazed.

"They are pretty wary by the time they get to the States, but these flew straight from the breeding grounds and arrived here yesterday," I tell him.

We discuss the rest of the day and opt for the thousands of ducks we see trading the shoreline a mile or so away. It could be a short day after all, and if we want more geese we can come back. Snows stashed as well, we slog off over the treacherous slime with decoy bags and over and under shotguns. As we get closer it becomes obvious that we should have brought the decoy bags empty to carry ducks in. The tide was almost at ebb, and with an offshore breeze the ducks, mostly blue-wing teal but also plenty of big ducks, were drifting and feeding along shore in shallow water. Great rafts at the end of the drift would pick up and fly the shore back to point A. There were thousands. We hid in the rocks and decided to call our shots. I was having one of those rare days when you can visualize the shot string intercepting the target. When they caught the crosswind the teal had to be going fifty. Not even this is a problem on this rare day. I ration my shots but even so my limit is over pretty quick. With the tide now coming back it was only necessary to walk down to the water and pick up the birds. Travis was burning lots of powder and had a ways to go to fill out.

"I may never have a chance to do anything like this again, and I am going to stay here until I fill the last one."

With six kids and an important position at a major ski company, his few yearly hunts are sacred. This group was here as my corporate guest, friends I was paid to entertain. I moved over to join him for encouragement and be his retriever.

"My God! What is that?"

Around the corner in a big inflatable came the pirate, Monsieur La Chance. A guide from an inhabited island, he had been poaching Ile Bature for decades. An unwritten agreement existed that he would not land when the camp was occupied; he could tell by the pennant on the flagpole. Mogy knew that there was nothing to prevent him from torching the place at will. At the same time LaChance was so notorious that other poachers feared to tread on his territory. What he was doing today broke every law, but he knew it would go unreported. Five guns were blazing as the boat screamed towards shore, ducks falling like rain and shot on the water. Every duck panicked and went airborne. They flew around us like mosquitoes and Travis easily took his last two legal ducks and our hunt was over.

Three Camps Plus One

With an equal mix of small and big ducks on stringers, the unnecessary bags of decoys, guns, ammo and bulky clothes, the fun part lay ahead; the forced march home. A slip and a landing on the razor-sharp gray shale sliced through my rubber waders, underwear and through my knee. Bloodied and almost bowed we hung our game in a shed named the Morgue and compared notes with the other party, which had not done as well. I bandaged my throbbing knee and retired to my stateroom for a nap.

Tonight my schedule was to prepare brandied snow goose stew. By the time these birds get to Texas they are called Sky Carp because their diet on the way south renders them inedible. Early in their journey they are not as delicious as Canadas, but they are fine fare if prepared thoughtfully.

With Travis as my sous chef, in the waning light we heard persistent gunfire from a tiny freshwater pond near the house where a few hundred ducks flew in to spend the night. In dimness and off the end of the gun barrel they were almost impossible to hit. The boys arrived.

"How many shells you shot?"

"Box and a half each."

"How many you hit?"

"Two."

Cocktail hour at Ile Bature is a leisurely affair. With no place to go and no conveyances, there is often a bit of refreshment taken during the day. The wind switched to the north as we traded tales around the stone fireplace in the main room, and by the last sip of wine and the last of the stew it was blowing a fair gale. There would be no leaving the island tomorrow. The boat would have to be moved to a safer mooring. Mogy's greatest labor of love was to design and build a twenty-four-foot dory on his lawn in Vermont to replace a less satisfactory and more risky craft. Loaded with as many as seven people and all their gear it was often an exciting and damp crossing both ways. Every swell looked like it was coming over the side. One man traveled from Connecticut, left in a mild chop and one hundred yards from shore ordered the boat turned around. He spent three days in a motel awaiting the return of his companions who did not value life as much as he did. Having crossed in the old boat in which the guides drowned and the new one I would not agree with its builder that it could not swamp, but it was a vast improvement. But there are times on this water when no one ventures forth and this was going to be one. J.D., who was well into the cocktails, had the unenvied task of calling home through a marine operator in Quebec City. The enforced extra day was suspect and interfered with social engagements at home. He started giggling at his wife's stern invective and pushed the transmit button at the wrong time as we guffawed in the background. Finally he said, "You're breaking up; you're breaking up!" as the tirades continued, and rang off.

There is little doubt that Ile Bature and the camp are haunted. Things move about, doors lock and voices howl in the night. With all the history, shipwrecks and departed family, the ghosts must work off a duty roster. The boat would have to be moved that night because of the wind shift and the force of the gale. Mogy and I suited up and walked into the storm. Around the point we spotted the ship's light, but not where it should be.

"Holy Jesus! The boat's dragging anchor and who turned the light on?"

We plodded through the flats, and ten yards before we grabbed her the light went out.

The three ingredients for a great camp are history, hard work and soul. The Whitney and the Whitman families had fishing camps

Three Camps Plus One

from the Adirondacks to inland Maine. Their last camps were taken over by entrepreneurs when the families gave them up. For over twenty years one has been run by a local man and his wife. It is twenty miles in the bush and home to that strain of large brookies that are almost impossible to find in Maine anymore, a few over twenty inches. The last time our group went the spirit was extinguished from the lodge. The man is a tireless laborer who worked year-long to maintain and improve it. In the winter he would go in by snowmobile or skis to shovel the roofs. Though he is a licensed Maine Guide and loves to fish, he has little chance. A pleasant fellow but taciturn, he never stopped doing things. His wife, who cooked and was the gregarious hostess, was gone.

"She just upped and left after we raised our kids. . . . We ran this camp together for twenty-three years" was all her husband said. He brought an old gal from town out to cook the same menu, but it didn't taste the same. When she wasn't cooking she sat out back smoking on a stool. The fishing was fine, but there was no soul. We did not go back this May.

Jones Pond Camp is another of those camps where the family arrived by train, horse and wagon and canoe with full staff for the summer. This is now an exclusive club of members mostly from Maine. It consists of a central building and a number of cabins along the shore. The outhouse sign above the half moon dubs it "Alvin's Harmonica"—no one could tell me why. I have been a guest twice. One of my hosts had his ashes spread there several years ago. Like most Maine ponds, the trout have shrunk and the water is polluted with trash fish. There are several outlying ponds as well, but without a key to the gate, access is tough. Tradition here is as thick as fog on the coast and fiercely defended.

Without Sam the place would be in ruins. Sam is imperious, grating and structured. He also is a doer and forces others to donate the necessary hard labor to at least stay even. He is in his mid-sixties and no successor has come forward. With no whip the future could be in jeopardy.

No Nuttin'

Since I wrote this last summer I revisited a camp in the Deep South on the Mississippi-Alabama border, stopping on the way north this March. The break was welcome as we still had a formidable distance in miles and culture. A black resident once said to me, "I don't know where north is but I know it's a long way from here."

Mentioned in an earlier chapter protected by the "No Nuttin'" sign from trespass, the camp is set on stilts in a cyprus swamp. Some wag since my visit years back has placed a phone booth, red and phoneless, on the bank of this extension of the Tennessee Waterway to amuse the pilots of the tugs hauling huge barges. Numerous campaign signs exhort voters to reelect a popular circuit judge to a fourth term. He is white in a district that has four blacks for every white and defeats black candidates. He has won again.

There has been a camp here since anyone remembers. Mr. Robert, the landowner, and friends had to rebuild it after a fire destroyed the previous building. The new one is on stilts and has a log veranda, rockers facing the river. I once sat here watching thousands of ducks trading the other shore. The woods are loaded with deer, squirrels and turkeys. The inside is southern comfortable with big tables, leather furniture and a stone fireplace. The main room and kitchen area are open and lends itself to big

Three Camps Plus One

family events and "Thirsty Thursday." This weekly gathering was started by Mr. Robert's father in World War II when rationing proclaimed Thursday meatless. The local men meet to this day, bringing fish, game, whiskey and stories. Traditions seem especially durable in the South.

What luck. I arrive at the farm office early. Mr. Robert regales me with tales of catfish farming on the way to pick up the crawfish. An amazing fact is that pelicans have moved one hundred miles inland to feed off the young fry. Robert is concerned that one hundred pounds of crawfish, roughly five per man, will not be enough. These first crawfish of the year are cooked in giant cauldrons, boiled with whole onions, potatoes, corn, and mushrooms in a highly seasoned broth. The men share labor, cost and cleanup. Once you learn how to shuck the crawfish with a deft wrist flick they can be consumed like peanuts.

The ages of the men span twenty to eighty, with a sprinkling of grandsons. One doctor remembers the first Thirsty Thursdays in the forties. He is talking about an absent regular's Drathar bird dog. "The only way that would be a bird dog would be if it had a wing on it."

The conversation is hunting, fishing, dogs, food and the old days. Professional sports, Ol' Miss football and great jokes assure there is never a lull. Quite early, around ten o'clock, they exit en masse, leaving me to savor a final glass on the porch with the lights off, the riverboats for company.

Clubs, no matter how old or exclusive, are not necessarily great camps. I have belonged to or guided at some of the best, but without wild fish and game they are merely preserves with private membership. The Antis love this setup because no matter what the acreage or the opulence of the facilities the members are confined and "killing tame critters" raised not from the wild rivers and woods but for sport. It is only a matter of time before the small, scrabble clubs can be done away with by insidious liberal legislation. At our camp here in Cape Breton we are anything but contained. We are subject to the screwy new gun laws the gun haters have recently imposed on Canada, and to the onerous and "aboriginy"-prone Department of Fish and Oceans' decrees from Ottawa. But we share the same chance at the salmon with any other bloke on these wild rivers. The little bit of hunting we do is guided, but not on a preserve.

Cape Breton Island is changing and the salmon runs are diminished. Big Rod, a piper who is said to have weighed thirty stone, showed up at the opening ceremony of the causeway connecting Cape Breton to mainland Nova Scotia. Rod was in full clan regalia to play his bagpipes. It was the mid 1950s and Rod had never been off the island. He declined to march across, stating that this bridge was the death knell for Cape Breton, and he would have no part of it.

Fifty years later the motor homes stream past below our camp June through October. In August the weight of the tourist traffic threatens to sink the island.

If still in operation in fifty years we might touch on great camp status. But in the meantime, standing on the deck last week, under the full moon with pilot whales passing so close we could hear them blow, and the blue hills behind us moonstruck, it was not at all shabby.

— 26 —

Moscow, Vermont • April 2001

On Dogs and Dying

Some say a capricious God created a bond of unconditional love between man and dog, and then granted dogs one-fifth the lifespan of their masters. I am not complaining, though a well-cared-for pair of hunting boots will last over fourteen years. My dogs have given me far more than I have given them, and for this I am grateful. Some sportsmen after the passing of a special dog give up, refusing to own another dog. This I could never do, but Lord it aches when I lose one.

Great dog stories and some not so great cover a variety of themes, but all inevitably end with the death of the dog. Their lives are so short that even a super dog like Algonquin, in a book of the same name by Dion Henderson, who also penned *The Waltons,* ends in sadness. This book is my favorite bird-dog story, but the hero shares the same fate with the mutt in the worst of canine scribbling. We, on the other hand, with three score years and ten, can divide our lives into sections; Winston Churchill 1916-1946, a far more interesting subject than the sad old man who passed away decades later in his nineties. A dog's biography is punctuated by its death, and writers handle the end with every emotion from mawkish sentiment to stoic denial. Few do it well, but when so done the writing can be very good indeed.

Playing the fifteenth hole myself, dogs I now own or puppies I train will outlive me. A sobering thought. Wish I could time my demise with the final bottle in my cellar and the last dog in my kennel, but probably not. The mourning will be experienced several more times. I hope it doesn't get any tougher. I grieved for F.C. Panda in many ways more than I did for my mother, who died around the same time.

This is not shaping up to be my millennium thus far; the edge is off my shooting and golf and Tweed IV's disappearance two months ago into the Texas prairie haunts my days and nights. I have almost convinced myself he was "beamed up." We searched for days and never found any remains or a trail. Sure he was just shy of his sixteenth year and failing. He did me a favor, I guess, but I wonder and grieve. And what horror it is to lose a talented young one, for dogs live in constant combat with disease, vehicles, hunting accidents and other animals all competing to take them even sooner than their allotted time.

Maurice Chambers is a rodeo champion, renowned bow hunter, guide, outfitter and friend. Though we hunters may enjoy a close relationship with our bird dogs, unmatched is the love and respect shared by men and their catch dogs in hand-to-hand combat with four-hundred-pound wild hogs. After giving up the search for Tweed, Maurice presented me with this fine example of dog obituary, reprinted with his permission.

Our Last Talk
by Maurice Chambers

"Ol' Lucky, you're gettin' old, you're worn out, you can't even walk from the house to the barn anymore. It's come time for you to move on to a better place, my friend.

"We've run a lot of trails together, and we've caught a lot of wounded deer and big hogs. I've saved your life a time or two, and you've probably saved mine many times, but now that's all over here on earth, and it's come time for you to move on. I'll just have to join you later.

"You've always done what I've asked of you, so I'll ask one last favor. Will you please just go off into the woods and lie down someplace? Don't make me have to watch you die a slow, agonizing death here around the house. Go on out there and be where you belong —in the woods where the hogs are."

Once I'd finished speaking, Lucky looked me square in the eye. I touched him on top of the head with the palm of my hand, and he turned and slowly walked into the dark. With a lump in my throat, I got up from my chair and went into the cabin where Jamie and I were living prior to the time we built our new house.

Next morning, Ol' Lucky was gone; he was nowhere to be found. Even though I walked and looked for several days, still no Lucky. It was over two months before I found his carcass. Though he had gotten so weak he couldn't walk from the house to the barn anymore, he had somehow made it over a quarter of a mile from the cabin to a low area in the creek where a tall stand of wolfweeds grow thick, a place where the wild hogs frequent each time they are in the area. This was a place that Lucky knew well, and it was almost as if this were the place he'd kept in mind for just this occasion.

Once I'd found him, I stood up and walked back to the cabin, then went to the barn and dug out a strong nylon bag, walked the quarter-mile back to the wolfweed patch and knelt down beside the remains and put them in the bag and said, "Come on, Ol' Friend, we're going home." I buried him across the pond from the place where the house is now built, in the meadow under a large oak tree. A place where the deer and turkey graze morning and evening. A place where the varmints, javelinas and wild hogs frequent so often. A place where I watch through a big picture window each day as I make the morning coffee, and thank God that I happened to be in this world when one of his most outstanding creatures was passing through—Ol' Lucky!

Enough said. Thanks, Maurice.

Every Dog Has His Day. Good Dogs Have Two. And...

This next is dedicated to My Father and to the great German Shorthairs we had in my youth. Thanks Dad . . .

A Prayer from an Old Shorthair
By Charles Rose
WILD ROSE GERMAN SHORTHAIRS • DUBLIN, TEXAS

*I waken from fitful sleep, legs jerking, low growls deep within
my chest;*
Tired eyes look down on a wrinkled graying muzzle;
*With effort I roll, looking at gnarled scarred feet and legs
bearing a million old cactus spines buried within;*
Reminding me of all those prickly pear and jumping cactus.
*Slowly I lift my weary head and gaze upon a graying, cloud-
filled November sky;*
Deeply I breathe in . . . ahhh . . . finally . . . fall is here!!!
Longingly I gaze into the heavens above.
*Lord, please grant my master the strength to make one more
season;*
Twelve years have passed since our first hunt together . . .
*I have led him through cactus and mesquite, tall grass, rocks
hills and creeks.*
*We have seen together ten thousand covey rises, a thousand
cackling roosters and a million ducks taking flight.*
*But now, as I look in the window . . . I see my loving master
has tired . . . his pace has slowed and his once commanding
voice raspy and faded.*
*Lord . . . three lifetimes now have I pointed his quail, flushed
his roosters, marked his ducks . . . and brought them all to
hand . . . well most anyhow, and the few I ate . . . well he
didn't really want them anyhow.*

But time has caught us both . . . now he is slow to rise from his rocker as am I from my pad . . . his weathered face and my clouded eyes . . . neither the same as before . . . but still the lines in his face are maps I follow in my dreams . . . when clearer eyes led the way through green briar and snow . . . sandstorms and blinding rain.
Oh Lord grant us one more season so that as we each pass from this life we may pass on to our sons and daughters the life, the love, the joy and the sorrows of a thousand hunts we've shared.
And Lord, finally when the season is done would you grant him a soft chair, and me a fine rug . . .
By the hearth in your heavenly lodge . . .
Please Lord, Please, Just one more season . . .

Inspired by Duke, J.D., Bubba, Rocky and Killer.

It is with the heaviest of hearts I must add another to this list. On Saturday, October the sixth at around four A.M. the greatest friend, companion and hunting partner a man could have in this life left me. This will be the first season in 12 years that I've had to walk the fields without my her. All I can say is wait for me Rags and keep watching over the pups for me when I'm away. Thank you Rags for so many years.

—Charles Rose . . . Never your master, always your friend and partner.

On Dogs and Dying

August 2001

Five days ago my Mildred of Wild Rose was killed in the road. A chain of stupid events had lured her off the property she never left to her death on Route 100, Vermont's Cross-Bronx Expressway.

Her remorseful executioner was a fellow late for his golf date and talking on his cell phone in his SUV. I didn't see it happen and she should not have been there. Her killer offered to pay the cost of the dog. I declined. But could he please put back the heart he ripped from my chest?

I remember as a child being fascinated by the World War II honor roll that most small towns erected on their village green. Killed in action names rated a gold star next to them. Under L were four with the same name with these gold stars; all brothers, all Marines, all killed within a year in action in the Pacific. In a risky scheme such as this what's a couple of dogs? My hat is off to you, Mrs. Lapsley.

— 27 —

WATERBURY CENTER, VERMONT • AUGUST 1992

"Getting Together"

It's not getting any easier to take Spaniel and gun afield in quest of game in the wilds. Ignorance of what we do is rampant, and one hundred or more antigun and animal-rights groups promote the confusion to swell their coffers and gain support. Like "Defens" in the movie *Falling Down* it's so easy to be the bad guy.

Friendships made while trialing are often lasting. Bill Winney; longtime handler, judge, trial gun and bird planter extraordinaire was here in Vermont for woodcock in October. I'll visit him in Texas for dove and quail in January. A fine arrangement.

Continental Airlines played three-card monte with Bill's flight from Houston to Burlington, switching him to another airline and routing him through Detroit and Boston. Continental is the airline that lost, for fourteen hours, one of my dogs en route to a trial. So when they told me Winney had vanished from their computer, I left a note telling him to check into a motel and I would see him in the A.M.

Finally, arriving at midnight he was puzzled to discover a paucity of rooms. He lucked out at the HoJo and questioned the night clerk, "It's too early for deer season or skiing. Are all the rooms taken by bird hunters?"

"Leafers," was the taciturn reply—the vernacular for the hoards of annual visitors gathering to view our foliage each autumn.

"Oh," said Winney, thinking "leafers" to be some migratory shore bird from Nova Scotia traveling south for his hunting enjoyment.

Vermont is a bastion of sorts for hunters and dog trainers, as is Texas. Imagine his dismay when the lady behind the counter at the local liquor store in Waterbury asked him what brought him north. "Huntin,' ma'am," replied Bill.

At this she shrilled, "Think about the fact you are invading poor wild creatures' environment in an attempt to murder them."

I, who pay no attention to these types, answered I would cease to consider her proposal as soon as I was through the store's door and onto the street.

Half a mile down a logging road in an extremely remote corner of our state we were busting alder cover. I was walking toward my car. Tweed IV and Bill were still hunting to my left. To my wondering eyes appeared three Leafers dressed in white K-mart ski parkas and low-top shoes. To them the lone hunter advancing towards my NRA-sticker-covered '83 Chevette was straight out of *Deliverance*.

"Moose?" chirped one of the women.

"What?" I asked.

"Are you shooting the deers?"

I turned to my car muttering to myself that I always hunt them out of season with birdshot and dogs. Simultaneously, Winney popped out of the cover. Bill was not born in Texas but he could have been. Six-three and 280 pounds. He fought as a heavyweight boxer in his youth. This jovial teddy-bear of a man could appear menacing if he popped up at you. Tweed bounced out right next to them; a fifty-pound Springer covered with mud, looking every bit the Stephen Spielberg "Swamp Thing."

"Woodcock, ma'am." says Bill, brightly. Our Leafers stopped in their tracks.

"Oh Charles, let's go quickly." squeaked the woman. "They're talking dirty and they're carrying guns!"

Executing an about-face that would gladden the heart of a Marine Corps drill team sergeant, they scurried down the path at quick time.

"What did I do?" asked Bill.

— 28 —

HOLLOWVILLE, NEW YORK • APRIL 2002

Death of a Woodcock Cover and Leaving Vermont

Vermont in the sixties has been described as a "sandbox filled with snow." Alpine skiing facilitated by improved equipment was in its greatest growth phase. Skiers flocked to Vermont and some stayed as much for the hunting and fishing as the skiing. I was one. Trout abounded and the grouse and woodcock were phenomenal. There were so many ducks on Lake Champlain at times that I would forget shooting and simply count the flocks in the sky. Being a solitary type, I prefer hunting alone with just my dog or with one close friend—woodcock shooting for me is mystical. There were so many coverts within a twenty-minute drive that I would leave one and have difficulty deciding where to hunt next. There was a back road between Waterbury Center and Stowe with more coverts on it than you could hunt in a day. About equidistant from the two towns was Peter's and my favorite. There was a late square Victorian in the Grant Wood style with a cupola, which must have been the farmhouse. The property had been sold off and the house was for sale with a mere two acres before it burned. The cover was only about ten acres on both sides of a farm road. The left side was a bit too wet, though there were a few birds there during a flight. The right was perfect for native birds, and when the flights came in, the earthworm-rich soil kept them around. We always shot our last woodcock of the season there. I had little cause to travel this road except for hunting, but one summer day I decided to take the scenic route and to check the apples in a tiny pocket across the road from this cover that always held grouse. My God! A house and road were under construction above the alders, the angry red-posted signs were already in place, and worst of all, inexplicably, they were bulldozing and burning the alders. For what purpose they were destroying this great habitat I could only guess. Perhaps the owners were uncomfortable living above a swamp, preferring a more pastoral vista. I felt sick. That autumn we hunted the left side with no luck; our cover was dead. Recently I saw the brush struggling back. Since that time along this road and in the fingers and hollows off it a murderer's row of architectural horrors has sprung. Peter refers to them as ridgeline trophy houses, many of them enormous and ill suited to the sites on which they perch. Their architects should be condemned to live in them for eternity.

    It was time for me to leave. Peter says I am pursued by demons, and I guess this is true. I am out of sync with present day Vermont, politically and personally. I still return and will continue to visit some of the remoter places, which are pretty well unchanged. In past times during mud-season, when there is little to do, I would spend the time happily in a pub with all the attendant activities associated with such places. Neither I, nor my liver, can do this any longer, so these days drag by like dead animals until cocktail hour. I moved this hallowed time up from five o'clock to four. Maxie's market, run for fifty years by him behind the meat case and his wife and store cat at the front counter, is for sale. Some enterprising individual will turn it into yet another (in)convenience store. As a parting gift my Mildred the shorthair was killed by a SUV on Route 100, which now has up to fourteen thousand cars travel it a day between the two towns. And last fall in one of my few "hallowed" local covers was a gaggle of hunters behind two ill-trained Brittanies with those dreadful beep collars around their porcine necks.

How could I move to New York State? The answer is that the state is so vast and varied that Chuck and Hillary were urban-elected, not by my neighbors in rural Columbia County. Vermont politics are personal but here I don't care. I have two camps and three small outbuildings on four acres on a private gravel lane. It suits my budget and my requirements for solitude. The unposted land that is across my little stream is populated by turkeys; the season will open the end of this month. Certainly this property is not for everyone, but it suits me at this time in my voyage. My dogs like it here too.

Thirty minutes south is a kennel I have been training at for twenty-plus years with a friend, serial "marry-her" and genius dog trainer. Dog club activities and numerous shooting clubs make this region Spaniel Central. There are ducks on the Hudson and a plethora of geese resident and migratory. Although the grouse cycle is down to nothing, the woodcock are already back, and plentiful. But when late October comes I am sure my restless spirit will trudge back to those few old remaining woodcock covers that so captured my soul, to hunt them with an old friend.

— 29 —

HOLLOWVILLE, NEW YORK • OCTOBER 2002

Not Martha Stewart's Kitchen

If this book serves as any use at all, it should be that you should enjoy a few good meals. Early on it became apparent to me that I would need to cook. My mother, an indifferent cook at best, would attempt the few fish I caught or the small game I shot with my air rifle. She did this out of love, not with any hopes of making it edible. My grandmother, an instinctive and wonderful southern cook, would shun the pathetic offerings I brought, "Game...horrors!," she would exclaim. Women universally overcook anything wild to a gray texture, bloodless and dental proof. They say overcooking "gets rid of the gaminess," although I believe it is some sort of revenge against their harvester husbands. Invariably the best dishes of fish and game are prepared by the harvester.

Fish and game cookbooks abound. Over the years I have collected a library; some good, some bad, but all at least have a few useable recipes. When people can think of nothing to give me they buy me a cookbook. In general the recipes are either too simple—"Cover pheasant breast with a can of mushroom soup and simmer until done"— or so elaborate with exotic ingredients and arduous preparation instructions as to daunt Paul Bocuse. Over the years I have garnered, embellished, innovated and borrowed. These dishes have been tested for years and are not complicated or rigid in formula.

Canada Goose. Not many years ago a Canada was considered a prize, a holy grail of waterfowl said to be so intelligent that hundreds of decoys had to be placed just so. One neophyte goose hunter was convinced to walk backward through the snow to his blind so the geese would think he had left it. Now the damned things are everywhere. One has to kick them away from his golf ball. Some do not migrate, instituting resident "nuisance hunting seasons."

Dennis, the most ardent goose hunter I know, defies anyone to tell the difference between the travelers and the residents. We even select the young and tender ones to shoot, allowing the tough old warriors to fly away. Any goose recipe is dependent on bird quality and a cooking temperature of 325 degrees. Let your meat thermometer or your eye tell you when the bird is the color of medium-rare roast beef. If you wish a glazed skin a bit crisp, baste and apply a mixture of mustard and breadcrumbs, then turn up the heat for the last 20 minutes. Note that this and all subsequent recipes call for a plucked bird, not skinned. The extra effort is worth it.

Sauce Maugron. For the goose or gander—in my lexicon, *maugron* is the appellation for any sauce with no name. Pit and strain a one-pound can of purple plums. Reserve juice and puree fruit in blender. Sauté ¼ cup chopped onion in ¼ cup butter, then add plums and juice and a shot of gin. To the mixture add one tablespoon each of lemon juice, chili sauce (not ketchup), ½ teaspoon ground ginger, one teaspoon of Worcestershire, ¼ cup of brown sugar. Simmer and stir frequently for 30 minutes. If timed just right with further gin imbibed; the goose, the sauce and you will be done at the same time.

Woodcock. I am not proud of the numbers of these birds I used to shoot, and I fervently pray that God is not a woodcock. It is already late October and I have not been in the woodcock coverts yet. But autumn and the flight will not pass before I shoot a brace or two for my own consumption.

Those who detest the bird say they taste like liver. For me the plump dark breast with visible fat on the skin (again ... the bird is plucked, not skinned) in concert with the delicate white meat legs makes these birds my favorite. The controversy revolving around hanging the bird English way is to me moot. I like to prepare them the day they are shot.

Woodcock with Ginger and Currant Sauce. In a pan on the stovetop melt ½ stick butter or, if you prefer, use ½ cup olive oil. In it sauté copious chopped garlic, fresh parsley and chopped ginger root. To this add the birds and some sherry (or gin if you wish). Keep turning and basting until done to your wishes, and test with knife or fork. Some barely cook woodcock, but I'll pass, preferring them the texture of medium-rare steak, which for me is about ten minutes on my stovetop. About halfway through add generous dollops of black currant jelly. Serve on toast. I went through a period when I used to bake the trail (innards) separately to put on the toast. One time I got a mouthful of swamp flavor and sand, which turned me away, for good. "*Chacque à son gout.*"

Teal. There are so many recipes for pheasant, most work as those for chicken, so I will not waste space on them here. Now, these smallest of ducks, or you can substitute wood duck, are a different matter. Once again I use whole birds, skin on.

Yankee Teal Italian. My southern friends are amazed a Yankee can actually cook. I temper the blow by telling them about my southern grandmother. Sauté birds in olive oil with an onion and chopped garlic. In a covered dutch oven or roasting pan add one can of crushed Italian tomatoes, sliced black olives, a tablespoon of lemon juice. Put in the ducks and layer with cilantro. Cook for 45 minutes in a 350-degree oven. Notice there is no booze in this dish. My friends call martinis "Yankee whiskey." They make a fine aperitif.

Quail. John Y. recently retired after forty years with the New York State Department of Environmental Protection. Largely through his efforts the wild turkey was reintroduced with amazing success. John is a keen hunter of every imaginable bird and animal available in this vast state. He also is an estimable chef, an art he learned in his family's restaurant in the Catskills. Besides, he is a prodigious eater. The one game bird not indigenous to his state is the quail, so those we shoot are pen-raised. Even so, the piquant flavors of this recipe come through. I have six or so on hand, which will be devoured this week. This is one of the few meals for which I claim no authorship. It is too good to embellish.

Quail with White Grapes and Champagne. Split quail, roll in flour and brown in butter. Add one cup of champagne, fresh button mushrooms and split seedless white grapes. Cover and simmer on the stovetop for ½ hour. That is it. No extra herbs, and do not substitute white wine or woodcock.

Doves. My Texas pals laugh when I pluck doves. I can do this almost as fast as they can pop out the breasts. The marinade is a meeting of two worlds—a good but not over powering hot sauce, olive oil, fresh lime juice and Vermont maple syrup. The proportions are up to you. Shoot the doves in the morning and let them soak for the afternoon and grill them in the evening in the field on a mesquite fire while enjoying tequila and iced Pacificos. No eating utensils are required except for the beans, gaucamole and flour tortillas. Three per hunter is the bare minimum, but I have witnessed a dozen consumed without a qualm.

— Afterword —

Storing Lasts

My first two lasts I recall were both around my fiftieth birthday. One was my last game of squash racquets, the other my last spring-skiing trek up Mt. Washington with several kids in tow. We were attacked by blackflies, which came out of the snow of all things, biting one little camper enough to give him blood poisoning. It was time for me to ease off these activities and concentrate more on hunting and fishing. Lasts need not be athletic; it could be a final drink and a meal at a favorite club or restaurant. I will always remember a must-stop at a friend's quintessential southern restaurant in Meridian, Mississippi. Over one hundred years old with an octagenarian waitstaff, the memorabilia on the walls told the history of the Old South. The counter was over one hundred feet with booths on the other wall. And lord, the catfish they fried up and two-and-a-half-ounce bourbons they poured! But the new south has no use for these anachronisms. The décor is now California fern bar, the ancient black staff replaced by, "Hi, I'm Chip your server."

All lasts need not be invidious or sad. A man was consumed by his passion for hunting ducks; for years his business and home life suffered. One day he quit cold his addiction. A partner would come by and taunt him with tales of limits bagged and glorious days of hunting he was having.

"It wasn't so bad," he told me. "On the days he was freezing his toes in the marsh I was at his house in bed with his wife."

I received my Medicare card in the mail last week, but I have been storing memories for some time to use in an emergency when my strength goes. Old age isn't for sissies. There's the long walk back with Arrow after she completed the final series of a National Championship, beating out 120 of the best Spaniels in the world. I recall every detail of that November day on the rolling western New York hillsides.

A misty morning at a Scottish estate with all the beaters, dogs and shooting companions bustling about prior to leaving for the first drive.

Letting the dogs out at 6 A.M. with a full Iowa moon over the native prairie grass on Frank and Genny's farm, which I have hunted for a dozen years or more.

A final point by a paperless, broken-tail Pointer named Uno in a Texas cow pasture. One of the famed "Pointer brothers" whose sibling died last year. Leighton and I, hunting without clients, taking a pair of quail at day's end over what we jokingly called the "A Team." Uno, three years ago my Mildred's bracemate, is backed by my Spaniel, Arrow, at "hup."

Afterwards at the rig—cheap scotch and rich talk.

Shooting, fishing and skiing moments shared to this day with young sportsmen I mentored, and with old friends. Sometimes the magic was the lightness of fresh powder, or the excitement of a mayfly hatch, but always the comradeship linked the moment.

But I'm not quite ready for the armchair, and there is more storing to do. See you at the end of the hedgerow.